Big Book of
Botanical Crafts

COFFEE
MASSAGE
BAR

honey
dandelion
lip
scrub

Big Book of
Botanical
Crafts

How to Make Candles, Soaps, Scrubs, Sanitizers & More with Plants, Flowers, Herbs & Essential Oils

Stephanie Rose
garden therapy

BETTER DAY BOOKS®
HAPPY · CREATIVE · CURATED

Publisher: Peg Couch
Editor: Colleen Dorsey
Cover/book designer: Ashlee Wadeson
Production design: Lori Ehrlich
Photo stylists (Home Apothecary and Creative Candles content):
  Lori Wenger and Stephanie Rose
Photographers (Home Apothecary and Creative Candles content):
  Jason Masters and Stephanie Rose
Photo stylist and photographer (Soaps & Sanitizers content):
  Stephanie Rose
Photos on pages 4–5, 6–7, 9, and 74–75: Styled Stock Society; photo on pages 132–133: Getty Images/wera Rodsawang; design on endpapers: Shutterstock/Oksancia
Author photos on pages 2 and 14:
  Susan Goble/Wildflower Photography

Library of Congress Control Number: 2022937959

ISBN: 978-0-7643-6545-4

Printed in China

First printing

Copublished by Better Day Books, Inc., and Schiffer Publishing, Ltd.

The information in this book is not advice and should not be treated as such. Any reliance you place on such information is strictly at your own risk and not a substitute for medical, legal, or any other professional advice of any kind. What is written in this book is not intended to be substituted for the advice provided by your doctor or other healthcare professional. If you have any specific questions about any medical matter, you should consult your doctor or other professional healthcare provider. The author and publisher specifically disclaim all responsibility for any liability, loss, or risk, personal or otherwise, that is incurred as a consequence, directly or indirectly, of the use and application of any of this content. The views expressed in this book have not been reviewed or endorsed by the FDA or any other private or public entity. The author and the publisher urge all readers to thoroughly review each project and to understand the use of all materials before beginning any project. Take precautions to protect pregnant women, children, and pets when using essential oils.

MIX
Paper from responsible sources
FSC® C167893

BETTER DAY BOOKS®

Better Day Books
P.O. Box 21462
York, PA 17402
Phone: 717-487-5523
Email: hello@betterdaybooks.com
www.betterdaybooks.com
@better_day_books

SCHIFFER PUBLISHING

Schiffer Publishing
4880 Lower Valley Road
Atglen, PA 19310
Phone: 610-593-1777
Fax: 610-593-2002
Email: info@schifferbooks.com
www.schifferbooks.com

This title is available for promotional or commercial use, including special editions. Contact info@schifferbooks.com for more information.

This book is dedicated to you.

Yes, you. You are a beautiful, creative gift to this earth. You gave yourself the gift of spending moments enjoying the wonder of plants and making wonderful things. And now you can say you have a book dedicated to you! Truly know that without you, this book wouldn't have been made.

– xoxo

8
Introduction
Creative Wellness 10

Meet the Author 14

16
Home Apothecary

GETTING STARTED 18
Botanical Bath Salts 26
Tub Tea 30
Herbal Foot Soak 34
Floral Bath Bombs 38
Lavender & Cocoa Butter Bath Melts 42
Coffee Bean Massage Bars 46
Calendula Lotion Bars 50
Double Chocolate Mint Lip Balm 54
Honey Dandelion Lip Scrub 58
Peppermint Coconut Sugar Scrub 62
Healing Himalayan Pink Salt Scrub 66
Aromatherapy Perfume 70
BOTANICAL BATH TIME 74

76
Creative Candles

GETTING STARTED 78
Warming Cappuccino Candle 88
Clay Pot Citronella Candles 92
Citrus Celebration Wax Melts 96

100 Herbal Sleepy Time Wax Melts
104 Healing Crystals Candle
108 Jam Jar Candle Favors
112 Lavender Candle
116 Summer Flowers Floating Candles
120 Seashell Tea Lights
124 Ombré Evergreen Candle
128 AROMATHERAPY

130
Soaps & Sanitizers

132 GETTING STARTED
140 Basil & Bergamot–Scented Moisturizing Liquid Hand Soap
144 Lime & Rosemary–Scented Foaming Hand Soap
148 Aloe & Witch Hazel Hand Sanitizer Gel
152 Alcohol-Based Hand Sanitizer Spray
156 Travel Disinfecting Wipes
160 Orange & Sage All-Purpose Cleaner
164 Lemongrass & Pine Alcohol-Based Disinfecting Kitchen Cleaner
168 Reusable Lemon & Rosemary–Scented Kitchen & Bathroom Wipes
172 Fruit & Vegetable Wash
176 Tea Tree & Peppermint Toilet Bombs
180 KEEPING THINGS FRESH

Herbal Appendix 182

Resources 186

Index 186

Introduction

I'm so proud of you! By sitting down with this book, you are doing something radical. Something revolutionary. Something beautiful.

Nurturing yourself.

While we know full well that it's critically important to our well-being to spend some time de-stressing and taking care of our bodies and minds, it is frequently too far down the to-do list. We forget about ourselves, our need for self-care. It often takes a caring friend or family member to remind us to slow down and look after ourselves in the way we would for others. Sometimes, our bodies are the ones to tell us that we need time to regenerate, through disease, injury, fatigue, pain, or emotional strain.

That's how I got started with herbalism and garden therapy. My body said that it was time to slow down, in the most inconvenient way. Overnight, I went from my corporate director-level position to being confined to bed for almost two years. To forge my path to wellness, I looked at every aspect of my life to see how I could make it simpler and more supportive. Of course, the first thing we often think about is what we put into our bodies, as well as how we spend our time. These are certainly important aspects of self-care. But what often goes overlooked are the products we use on our bodies and in our homes.

I started experimenting with plant-based oils, waxes, botanicals, and natural ingredients to replace the unrecognizable ingredients found in many store-bought skincare and housecleaning products. Once I learned some basic recipes, I was hooked. From just a few ingredients—many of which I had in my kitchen or garden—I was able to make a wide variety of wholesome products. And I was astonished by how different I felt. The balms made my skin silky, and the herbal baths eased away stiffness. My cleaning routine was simplified using natural housecleaners and soaps. And I discovered a new passion for creating natural candles that create ambiance.

And the best part? The act of making these products is not only easy, but also fun! Working with herbs and flowers is quite therapeutic. Experimenting with recipes is highly enjoyable. The act of doing these "jobs" feels more like self-care to me, and I hope you find the inspiration you need in these pages to fall in love with botanical crafting too.

This book presents 32 botanical craft projects that cover a range of functions, from cleaning, perfuming, and scrubbing to soaking, disinfecting, and simply enjoying. It is divided into three sections, each with its own easy-to-comprehend info for beginners who are new to crafting these kinds of products. You will learn to make skin and body products, candles, and cleaners that will allow you to reconnect with nature and eliminate harsh chemicals from your daily routine. The projects themselves are super easy and require mainly tools and ingredients that you may already have at home. Plus, they are highly customizable—you can effortlessly adapt the herbal ingredients to create a scent profile that you love.

My hope is that the projects in this book will give you an appreciation for time well spent, a connection with the healing power of plants, and a whole lot of self-care. Wherever you are on your personal journey, I'm thrilled to be accompanying you along the way.

Note about Measurements

The first time you try each recipe, I recommend using the precise measurements as they are listed so you can get the feel for how the recipes are intended to turn out. For best results, avoid converting measurements to different systems (such as milliliters to cups) unless an equivalent is already provided. With experience, feel free to experiment with substitutions—you could very well have some interesting and fun results!

Creative Wellness

Welcome to wellness through combining the healing power of plants with your unique creativity. I am just tickled that you picked up this book! Not only are you going to learn how to make a wide variety of botanical skincare products, candles, and cleaners, but you will also embark on an artistic journey that will nurture your mind, body, and soul.

We all know that crafting is fun, but did you know that crafting is also good for you? Studies have shown that making things by hand can reduce stress and anxiety, build self-esteem, and even improve cognitive function. So whether you want to calm your mind from the pressures of a busy life, make a gift for a friend or family member, or simply infuse your world with something beautiful, crafting is a healthy outlet that anyone can enjoy.

Here are some of the top benefits of exercising your creativity that you will surely enjoy through making the projects in this book.

1. IT'S YOUR TIME TO SHINE

When was the last time you did something just for yourself? If you are like most people, it may have been awhile. Being creative is "you" time. While the projects in this book offer specific instructions, I've left plenty of room for creativity. Once you master the techniques, I encourage you to make up your own recipes. Think about what botanicals you prefer and how to package your creations for gift giving. Maybe you'll use your new skills to start a craft business by selling your items online, at a craft fair, or at a farmers' market. You could give your items unique names, design cute labels, and make up a fun brand name. Expressing yourself authentically in this way is fun, builds confidence, and lets your uniqueness shine.

2. MAKE HEARTFELT CONNECTIONS

One of the best things about crafting is the connection that it creates when shared. Imagine gathering around a table with a group of people you love, laughing, crafting, and making something wonderful. While hands are busy, conversation flows, and we can connect with one another in a different way. Catch up with your friends, make memories with a special child in your life, or invite the neighbors over. Organizing a crafting event does not have to be a fancy affair—in fact, it's way more fun if it's not! Put the teakettle on, throw an old tablecloth over the table to protect it, and have fun arranging the craft materials. Many of the projects in this book are perfectly suited to being made outdoors, too, so have a garden party and let nature inspire you and your guests. It's the perfect setting to make botanical crafts!

3. RELEASE THE STRESS

Crafting is an incredible outlet for emotions and a great opportunity to practice mindfulness. You will be working with many natural materials when making the projects in this book, so take time to utilize all of your senses as you work. Notice how the materials feel, and inhale the fresh aroma of the herbs and essential oils. Be in the moment as you craft and notice your breath slowing down. Focus on each step one by one without worrying about the end result or whether you're doing it "perfectly." Crafting gives us a chance to be present in a world where we are constantly bombarded with incoming information, a chance to be mindful of how your brain and body can work together to create something that didn't exist before *you* made it. Nurture the creativity within you, and you'll notice a positive impact on your life.

4. BUILD YOUR BRAIN

You do not need to be a master crafter to experience the positive cognitive benefits of crafting. Even the simplest crafts can help to improve your focus. Have you ever been so engrossed in doing something creative that you lost all sense of time? Psychologist Mihaly Csikszentmihalyi calls that experience "flow." Being in a state of flow is similar to meditation and is considered one of the purest forms of happiness. It has also been shown to help with memory and attention span, visuospatial processing, creativity, and problem-solving. According to a study published in the *Journal of Neuropsychiatry*, crafting could reduce your chances of developing mild cognitive impairment by 30% to 50%. So, enjoy making the projects in this book and allow yourself to get into a state of flow. Your brain will thank you for it.

Since this book is focused on botanical crafting, you're getting a double bonus of these feel-good benefits. Working with healing herbs, growing your own plants, and enjoying their beautiful aromas has a host of health benefits that I share throughout these pages. It has given me great joy to develop and perfect these recipes, and I hope you will enjoy making them over and over. Have fun and be creative—it's good for you!

Meet the Author
Stephanie Rose

is an award-winning author, gardening expert, certified permaculture designer, herbalist, and wellness advocate. After Stephanie faced her own debilitating illness, she found solace and healing through gardening and herbs. Now, she draws on experiences from her personal journey and expert garden knowledge in her books and popular website, Garden Therapy®. Stephanie has written 12 published books on creative gardening, permaculture, herbalism, and natural beauty. As a Vancouver Master Gardener, she volunteers to develop children's gardens to help our littlest gardeners fall in love with the earth. Stephanie continues to lovingly dedicate her life and her work to her community around the world, encouraging healing, wellness, and the joy of gardening. Discover more at *gardentherapy.ca.*

Home Apothecary

A little pampering is key to good self-care.

A soak in a warm tub filled with flower petals can soothe skin while giving the mind a much-needed break. A massage from a loved one can foster connection while easing aches and pains. The herbal therapy of botanicals can help with ailments from tired feet to lack of focus. The handcrafted herbal recipes in this section of the book will help you prioritize the sentiment of self-care. As a bonus, they also make great gifts!

You can curate a veritable home apothecary filled with natural ingredients that can be made into a variety of lotions and potions. Flowers, cocoa butter, plant oils, beeswax, and essential oils can make an abundance of homemade products that all draw on the healing power of plants in the most beautiful way possible.

Plus, there is plenty of room to play around with customizing your creations based on your personal tastes. By keeping the basic ingredients the same, but switching out the fragrances and the botanicals used, you can make a completely different project. It's great fun to invent different blends, and even more fun to do the testing. So, try out each of the projects presented here and spend some time pampering yourself in the process!

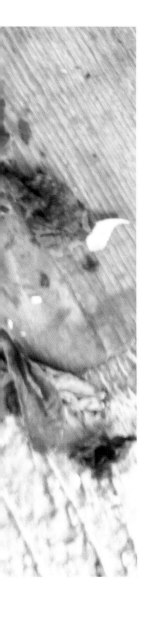

Getting Started

Anyone can make gorgeous and healing bath and body products from natural, plant-based ingredients. These tried-and-true recipes are suitable for beginners, safe for children, and easy to scale up for large quantities (like wedding favors). The recipes are easy to follow and simple to customize. By changing up the botanicals, herbs, and essential oils, you can create a completely different product that uses the same base recipe.

There are two methods for making the projects in this section:

MEASURE AND MIX: Measure the ingredients, stir, and add the mixture to a container.

MELT AND POUR: Measure the ingredients, melt over heat and stir, and then add to a container.

Both methods are easy, and the results are simply beautiful. The Measure and Mix method needs little explanation—you simply measure the ingredients and mix them together, and they are good to go. The Melt and Pour method is also incredibly simple, but it has one extra step: melting the ingredients over heat. This method is used to make lip balms, massage bars, lotion bars, and bath melts.

Equipment

The recipes are easy to make with standard equipment from your kitchen, like a double boiler, a kitchen scale, mixing bowls, and canning jars. You don't need a lot of equipment to make these products at home, but here are a few of the essentials.

KITCHEN SCALE

A kitchen scale is an essential part of measuring the ingredients for each of these recipes. It can be tempting to try to convert the mass/weight of the ingredients into volumetric baking measurements like cups and tablespoons, but I don't recommend doing this. The ingredients come in many different forms and therefore might have a different weight per volume. For example, both beeswax and cocoa butter can come in solid blocks or in pastilles. A solid chunk of beeswax or cocoa butter will take up less volume but weigh more than the pastilles would in a measuring cup. To get the right mix for each of these recipes, use a kitchen scale and you'll be pleased with the results.

DOUBLE BOILER

For recipes that use the Melt and Pour method, you will need either a double boiler or a microwave. I prefer a double boiler. You can use a traditional double boiler or make your own using a number of different things found in your kitchen, such as an electric pan filled with an inch or two of water and a heatproof container like a mason jar, measuring cup, or beaker.

You could also use a pot with a smaller pot or bowl set inside of it. The inner pot can be a small pot, recycled can, mason jar, Turkish coffee pot, metal or glass jug, or metal or glass bowl. The water pot can be a large pot, pan, or even a baking pan. Set the inner pot on a small metal trivet inside the water pot to keep it raised off the bottom of the water pot and the heating element.

MOLDS

To make bars, bath bombs, and bath melts, you will need various molds. You can buy round molds specifically made for bath bombs or make smaller (non-round) bath bombs in an ice cube tray. For melts and bars, silicone ice cube, candy, or soap molds work perfectly. There is such a wide variety available that you can certainly find a large selection of molds at a craft store or online.

Making Balms and Bars

Balms and bars come together using the Melt and Pour method by having the ingredients melted over moderate heat, stirred, and poured into a mold to harden. There are two ways of melting the ingredients together: the double boiler method and the microwave method.

THE DOUBLE BOILER METHOD

Double boilers come in many shapes and forms, but the general idea is to heat the contents of an inner pot in an outer pot filled with water. This will gently melt your ingredients, and it is often quicker and heats the ingredients more evenly than the microwave method.

1. Measure the ingredients into the inner pot and fill the outer pot with a few inches of water.

2. Use medium heat on most stovetops to keep the water in the outer pot warm, but not boiling.

3. Stir the ingredients regularly while they melt, and remove them from the heat as soon as the contents have liquefied. Overheating the ingredients can reduce their effectiveness and longevity.

4. Once the ingredients are melted and removed from the heat, add botanicals and essential oils, give it one more stir, and then pour into a mold to set.

THE MICROWAVE METHOD

The double boiler method is my preferred method for evenly and quickly melting ingredients. The recipes show double boiler configurations as examples. However, if you prefer to use the microwave, then follow these steps in place of the double boiler method listed in the recipe instructions. If you keep a close eye on the microwave, it can be a handy tool.

1. Measure the ingredients into a heatproof measuring cup, mason jar, or other container that is safe to use in the microwave.

2. Start heating the ingredients in thirty-second intervals for large batches and ten-second intervals for smaller batches, then check and stir the ingredients at ten-second intervals until the solids have liquefied. It's important to use the ten-second intervals because the ingredients can burn very quickly and ruin your project.

3. Once the ingredients are melted, add botanicals and essential oils, give it one more stir, and then pour into a mold to set.

Customization

The recipes in this section are proven to be marvelous blends, but if you want to switch them up, simply scale the recipe down and make a test batch with your substitutions. If you like the results, then go for it on a larger scale! If you don't, keep making adjustments until you find something you love.

Ingredients

Many of the ingredients required for the recipes in this book can be found right in your very own kitchen (or garden)! Some others will need to be specially purchased, but they are all easy to access online or in stores. All of the ingredients called for are organic, natural, and gentle on skin, but even so, it's best to test a small amount of any product beforehand to rule out allergies and sensitivities.

HERBS AND OTHER BOTANICALS

Many of the recipes call for fresh or dried herbs or flower petals. Harvesting plants from the wild or from the garden allows you to get in touch with nature and also harness the healing power of plants. You can always purchase dried botanicals if you can't find them fresh. Herbal tea is an excellent source for dried herbs. If you purchase herbs and botanicals, choose ones that are organic and culinary grade.

ESSENTIAL OILS

Essential oils are extracted from plants in a process that allows the purest essence of the fragrance and healing benefits to be captured in a tiny bottle. Many plants go into each bottle, so it's a very concentrated liquid, and you don't need to use a lot to make an impact in a recipe. When making projects using the Melt and Pour method, the essential oils are added just before the ingredients are poured to ensure they don't become overheated and evaporate in the melting process.

Expiration Dates

Expiration dates for homemade products vary depending on a few factors. If the recipe is made of plant oil, cocoa butter, beeswax, and essential oils, the product will last as long as the expiration dates of those ingredients. Look at the labels on the ingredients and determine which has the soonest expiration date—this is the date your homemade product will expire.

When ingredients like herbs, botanicals, sugar, and water are added, they move up the expiration date. A sugar scrub should only be used for a few weeks before being discarded. Any products that have water added to them (for instance, when they are used in the shower) will have a shortened shelf life. If you notice any signs of mold growth, odor, or discoloration, discontinue use immediately.

Vitamin E oil is an antioxidant that can be added to certain recipes to extend the shelf life of some oils. You would add just a little, typically 0.3%— 0.5%. If you are heating the recipe, add it last, after the oils and waxes have cooled. The best practice is to add vitamin E at the same time you add essential oils to a recipe.

PLANT OILS

OLIVE OIL: This is very common and easy to find (you probably already have a bottle in your kitchen!), so it's an accessible choice to use as an ingredient for homemade skincare products. In your skincare products, there's no need to use virgin/extra virgin olive oil, so keep the fancier stuff for cooking and use a good, basic olive oil in your home apothecary. Olive oil is quite heavy and can clog pores, so it's best for products that will not be applied to the face. Olive oil hydrates and conditions skin well. It will add a bit of a yellow-green color to products and can have a strong scent—mix it with other ingredients so it doesn't become overpowering.

GRAPESEED OIL: A byproduct of winemaking, grapeseed oil is made by pressing the natural oils out of grape seeds. The oil doesn't have much of an aroma and is very light, quick to absorb into skin, and full of antioxidants. Grapeseed oil is good for facial products and those with oily skin because it is so light and will hydrate skin without making it feel greasy.

CASTOR OIL: This oil comes from the castor bean and has emollient properties. Unlike other oils, castor oil creates a solid film on the surface of skin, which works to lock in moisture and keep skin hydrated.

SWEET ALMOND OIL: A result of pressing nuts from the sweet almond tree, this oil contains the same beneficial nutrients and fatty acids you get from eating almonds. The oil is light, with a sweet fragrance, and works to maintain regular pH levels in skin, making it an effective ingredient for use on normal to dry skin types. It also contains Vitamin E, which protects and softens skin. Note that sweet almond oil is not safe for those who have nut allergies.

COCONUT OIL: Coconut oil contains a high quantity of fatty acids, has antibacterial and antimicrobial properties, and smells like a tropical vacation. It is especially effective at moisturizing the skin when combined with other ingredients. Coconut oil is good for hydrating sun-damaged skin and helps prevent the look of aging. Unrefined, virgin/extra virgin coconut oil is best for use in homemade skincare products.

COCOA BUTTER: You guessed it—cocoa butter comes from cocoa beans. It is an edible fat and is the main, essential ingredient in chocolate, which is why it smells so delicious. It is wonderful for hydrating skin and contains antioxidants that you can absorb through your skin. Cocoa butter is a solid at room temperature, but heating it will transform it into a liquid that can be combined easily with other ingredients for a beauty recipe. Cocoa butter has a strong chocolate aroma that holds well in recipes. If you don't care for the scent, it can be purchased in a processed form that has the scent removed. The recipes in this book use organic, raw cocoa butter that adds a mouth-watering aroma to the end products.

OTHER INGREDIENTS

BEESWAX: This is used in a lot of beauty products because it works so well to bind various ingredients and create a more solid texture. It can be purchased in pastilles and solid blocks. Pastilles are the most convenient form because you don't have to grate them as you do the solid blocks, but they are also usually more expensive, so use the form that works best for you. When choosing beeswax for your home apothecary, make sure it is organic, cosmetic grade, and filtered. Unrefined, filtered beeswax has a heavenly honey scent that you will love.

EPSOM SALT: This mineral compound contains magnesium and can help relieve muscle pain. It has anti-inflammatory properties and works well as an exfoliator to remove dead, dry skin that can be itchy and uncomfortable.

How to Make Herb-Infused Oils

You can use any of the plant oils listed on the previous pages exactly as they are in the recipes in this book, or you can make herb-infused versions and use them in the same way to add a little extra fragrance, color, and healing power.

To infuse oil with botanicals, the oil needs to be heated to allow the properties of the herbs to transfer to the oil. There are three different heating methods you can use: a stovetop, a slow cooker, or the sun.

Whatever heating method you choose, the basic steps are to pack a clean container full of dried herbs, pour oil over the herbs to submerge them, heat, and then strain the herbs out of the oil. It is important to use completely dried herbs, since moisture can introduce bacteria and mold to the mixture.

My favorite oils to use for infusing are olive oil, grapeseed oil, and coconut oil. You can use any herbs that you like, but on the facing page are the ones I've found to work best.

When your infused oil is ready, store it in a container with a tight-fitting lid and keep it in a cool, dark location. Generally, infused oil will last up to the expiration date on the original oil's package label. Olive oil should last for two to three years, and coconut oil will last for many years, although spoiling could happen more quickly if contaminants are introduced during the infusing process.

HEATING METHODS

ON THE STOVETOP: Gently heat your herbs and oil in a double boiler on medium-low heat. If you are using coconut oil, heat it to liquefy it, then add the herbs. If you are using any other oil, first add your herbs to the double boiler, then pour the oil over top. Once the mixture is heated, turn the temperature to low and leave it for a few hours until it becomes very aromatic.

IN A SLOW COOKER: This method works well as long as you have a slow cooker with a very low heat setting. Add your ingredients to mason jars and place the jars inside the slow cooker. You do not need to add lids to the jars—just put the slow cooker lid on. Set the slow cooker to the lowest setting and leave it for eight to twelve hours. If the temperature in the slow cooker becomes too warm, raise the oil jars up on a trivet or a washcloth to diffuse the direct heat.

IN THE SUN: Fill canning jars with herbs and pour oil over top until the herbs are submerged. Put the lids on the jars and set them outside in the sun for about eight hours. Do this on a sunny day, but not at the peak of summer, since overheating the oils can remove some of their beneficial properties.

Herb Benefits

LAVENDER   *Antibacterial properties, soothing scent, adds a purple-brown color to oil*

CALENDULA   *Very gentle, heals skin, adds a golden color to oil*

CHAMOMILE   *Calming scent, antibacterial, helps clear up acne*

COMFREY   *Anti-inflammatory, pain relief*

SAGE   *Anti-inflammatory, reduces redness and wrinkles*

MINT   *Energizing scent, pain relief, adds a dark color to oil*

ROSE   *Increases skin's permeability, reduces discoloration and wrinkles, adds color to oil if rose petals have pigment*

Botanical Bath Salts

Makes three 85-gram (3-ounce) test tubes

There's nothing more healing than time spent soaking in a warm tub. Using botanicals, essential oils, and bath salts is a luxurious way to pamper your skin and detoxify your body. A trio of botanical bath salts allows you to choose from three unique healing baths for different moods. Lavender bath salts are wonderful before bedtime and allow your body to relax into a deep sleep. Rose (*Rosa* spp.) bath salts are soothing and help to repair skin, plus rose is the flower of romance. Citrus bath salts can help cheer you up when you've got the blues.

INGREDIENTS

- 270 grams (9.5 ounces) Epsom salt

RECIPE #1

- ¼ cup dried lavender buds
- 10 drops lavender essential oil

RECIPE #2

- ¼ cup dried rose petals
- 10 drops essential oil blend that includes rose

RECIPE #3

- ¼ cup dried citrus rind and zest
- 10 drops citrus essential oil blend or any combination of sweet orange, grapefruit, lime, lemon, tangerine, and bergamot

MATERIALS

- Three 85-gram (3-ounce) glass test tubes with lids or corks

EQUIPMENT

- Kitchen scale
- Funnel or scrap paper

Lovely Lavender

*Lavender (*Lavandula angustifolia*) has been added to baths since Roman times because of its antibacterial properties and pleasing scent. The fragrance of lavender is used in aromatherapy to calm and relax and is purported to aid insomnia, so choose lavender bath salts for a before-bedtime soak and settle in for a restful slumber.*

1 Gather all of your ingredients and set them out in your work area.

2 Using a funnel (or a sheet of scrap paper rolled into a funnel), fill each test tube with Epsom salt, leaving 1 inch of space at the top.

3 Pour the Epsom salt out of one of the test tubes into a small mixing bowl. Add the dried botanicals for Recipe #1 and mix to combine.

4 Use a dropper to add the essential oil for Recipe #1. Mix well and refill the test tube.

5 Repeat steps 3–4 with the ingredients for Recipe #2 and Recipe #3.

6 When you have filled all three of the test tubes with a different fragrance and botanical blend, top them with the corks or lids that they came with.

Package this trio of botanical bath salts in a set of glass test tubes, each topped with a cork. Wrap decorative wire around each test tube and toss in a dried bay leaf. Pop them into a burlap drawstring bag to give them as a set.

Tub Tea

Makes four 120-milliliter (approximately ½-cup) tub tea bags

Herbs are wonderful in the bath, but floating botanicals are not for everyone. Some people love to bathe in a sea of flower petals, while others may care for a more pristine bath. A tub tea allows you to give someone the full herbal bath experience without the botanicals to clean up after the water has drained. Using paper tea filters means that these tub teas can be tossed right in the compost bin after the bath.

INGREDIENTS

- 8 drops essential oil of your choice (optional)
- 1 cup Epsom salt
- 1 cup custom blend (see at right)

MATERIALS

- Four large paper tea filters

EQUIPMENT

- Sewing machine

Cleanse & Cure with Oatmeal

Oatmeal soothes skin and won't strip away the skin's natural oils, making it ideal for those with dry or sensitive skin. Oatmeal is a natural anti-inflammatory that can reduce pain and itching caused by sunburn, dry skin, and rashes.

BLEND INGREDIENTS

While the other recipes in this book are measured by weight, this recipe is measured by volume. Each tea filter will hold ½ cup of ingredients, half of which will be Epsom salt and half of which will be dried botanicals, herbs, salts, and other ingredients. Create a 1-cup blend using any of these ingredients that you would like to include.

- Ground oatmeal
- Powdered milk or goat's milk
- Baking soda
- Salts like Himalayan pink salt or Dead Sea salts
- Dried flowers like calendula, rose, or lavender
- Dried herbs like mint, ginger, or chamomile
- Dried spices like star anise or turmeric
- Dried herbal or green tea leaves

1 Select the ingredients you want to include in your tub tea and make a 1-cup blend.

2 Mix the Epsom salt and the blend of your chosen ingredients in a bowl or jar. If desired, add the essential oil of your choice and stir to combine.

3 Fill each tea bag with a few heaping spoonfuls of the mixture (about ½ cup).

4 Seal the tea bags by folding the top over a few times, and then use a sewing machine and a decorative stitch to sew the bags shut.

Tip: *The paper tea bags can be tossed in your compost bin after the bath so there is no messy cleanup. You could also package them in a cotton muslin drawstring bag for a reusable tub tea, but the remaining ingredients will need to be discarded and replaced after each bath.*

Use a letter stamp set and a gold pen to create a tag with the instructions "Add one bag to a warm bath." Attach the tags with mini wooden clothespins.

Herbal Foot Soak

Makes 475 milliliters (approximately 2 cups) of foot soak

Our feet work so hard for us—taking us on adventures, being squeezed into gorgeous shoes, and keeping us grounded. And yet, they often don't get the care they deserve. Soaking them in warm water with salts and botanicals is a quick and easy way to pamper your hardworking feet and give your whole body a bit of rest and relaxation. A foot soak can relieve muscle aches and stiffness, reduce inflammation, and improve circulation. It can also soften dry skin and deodorize your feet. But, more than anything else, it feels fantastic!

INGREDIENTS

- 2 cups Epsom salt
- 8 drops pure lavender essential oil
- 6 drops mint essential oil
- 2 drops eucalyptus essential oil
- 2 drops rosemary essential oil
- 1 teaspoon dried comfrey root powder
- ½ cup dried mixed flower petals, lavender buds, and mint leaves

MATERIALS

- Decorative glass jar
- Wooden scoop

Relieve Foot Pain

Since ancient Roman times (and probably before), comfrey root (Symphytum officinale) has been used to treat bruises, aches, and pains. It contains rosmarinic acid, an anti-inflammatory that can be a powerful tool for pain relief. Comfrey root also has a high content of allantoin, which stimulates new skin cell growth and soothes dry, itchy skin. Perfect for soothing tired, achy feet at the end of a long day!

1 Prepare your ingredients. Choose an attractive combination of botanicals to add color to the blend. They will steep in the warm water to add an herbal infusion. The bulk of the healing benefits come from the Epsom salt, comfrey root powder, and essential oils, so the mix of botanicals is up to you.

2 Fill a bowl with Epsom salt.

3 Add the essential oils and stir to combine.

4 Add the comfrey root powder and dried mixed botanicals.

5 Scoop the mixture into a decorative glass jar.

6 Add a wood scoop to the jar with the mixture before closing the lid.

Get Fresh

Sometimes feet start to smell like, well, feet. Eucalyptus, mint, lavender, and rosemary have natural deodorizing and antibacterial properties that can make feet feel and smell fresh again, even after a day trapped inside soggy boots or sweaty sneakers.

Creating a decorative clay tag for your jar is easy to do with air-dry clay. Roll out a 3" circle of terra-cotta air-dry clay until it is ¼" thick. Press a stem of flowers into the center of the clay, then roll over it gently with the rolling pin to really push it in. Remove the flowers and use a heart-shaped cookie cutter to cut out a heart with the flower imprint in the center. Use a skewer to make a hole at the top of the heart for twine. When the clay is dry, lightly brush the front with white craft paint. Tie jute twine around the jar a few times and attach the clay heart.

Floral Bath Bombs

Makes four 2½" round bath bombs

These homemade fizzing bath bombs will turn your bathtub into a hot tub. When skin-softening baking soda is combined with citric acid and added to the bath water, the effervescence disperses essential oils and botanicals into the water for an aromatherapy spa experience. Adding a few dried violets into the mold makes for an extra-special treat. Other dried flowers that would work well for a bath bomb include rose petals, calendula, chamomile, lavender, and bachelor's buttons.

There are many bath bomb recipes out there, but this one is the most consistently successful for me. I've found it's less about the ingredients and more about the technique. Follow the instructions carefully and you should have a set of gorgeous bath bombs on your hands.

INGREDIENTS

- 250 grams (8.8 ounces) non-aluminum baking soda
- 125 grams (4.4 ounces) citric acid
- 125 grams (4.4 ounces) organic cornstarch
- 125 grams (4.4 ounces) Epsom salt
- 100% pure witch hazel
- 20 drops grapefruit essential oil or a floral blend like rose, geranium, or lavender
- ¼ cup dried calendula petals
- Pressed, dried violets

EQUIPMENT

- Kitchen scale
- Small spray bottle
- Round, two-piece bath bomb mold

Natural Colorants

If you would like to add color to your bath bombs, use natural colorants and add them in small amounts before you add the witch hazel. Start with just a pinch of color and add more gradually as needed to get a deeper color. Keep in mind that any colorant will leave a residue on the bathtub, which means cleanup will be needed after the bath. These ground-up dried herbs and other organics work well as natural colors in bath bombs.

- GREEN: *spirulina, sage powder*
- GOLDEN YELLOW: *safflower powder*
- YELLOW: *turmeric*
- YELLOW-ORANGE: *annatto seed powder*
- RED-ORANGE: *paprika*
- PINK: *madder root*
- PURPLE: *alkanet (Ratan Jot)*
- BROWN: *cocoa powder*

1 Prepare the mold before you start working on your bath bomb so it is ready to use right away in step 5. Add a few flowers to the center of one-half of the mold, facing them toward the mold and away from you.

2 In a large bowl, add the baking soda, citric acid, cornstarch, and Epsom salt and mix well. Add the essential oil and mix again.

3 Using a small spray bottle filled with witch hazel, spray the surface of the mixture 6–8 times. Working quickly, blend the witch hazel into the mixture using your hands. Continue adding a few spritzes of witch hazel at a time and blending it rapidly until the mixture has the consistency of damp sand. It should feel dry but hold its shape when formed into a ball with your hands.

4 Add the calendula petals and mix them in with your hands.

5 Spray the flowers you added to the mold with witch hazel—just a tiny spritz to help them adhere to the bath bomb.

6 Working quickly, add the mixture to each half of the mold, firmly pressing it into the mold with your thumbs. Keep topping off the mix until there is no give at all when you press into the mold. You really want to pack the mixture in there tightly.

7 To finish, overfill each half of the mold and press the halves together firmly. Clean off any excess mixture that escapes from between the two mold halves.

Place the bath bomb in a wooden box with the flower facing up so you can see that pretty detail. Line the box with shredded paper printed with a message like "You are the bomb." To make the shredded message paper, repeat the sentence multiple times in a document with ample space after each paragraph, then print on decorative paper and cut the strips by hand. Crinkle the strips by folding them like an accordion, then use them to create a padded nest for the bath bomb.

8 Gently tap the outside of the mold to release the bath bomb. Carefully lay the bath bomb on a tray and let it dry, undisturbed, for twenty-four hours. Repeat steps 5–8 with the remaining mixture.

Troubleshooting

If your bath bomb crumbles, the mixture was too dry. If the mixture expands and fizzes, it is too wet. If the bath bomb sticks to the mold or cracks as it dries, the mixture may be too wet. The trick to mastering bath bombs is to get the mixture to the right consistency. Once you have the technique, making bath bombs is easy.

Lavender & Cocoa Butter Bath Melts

Makes 12 small bath melts

Warning: the mouthwatering scent of these luxurious bath melts may make you want to eat them. Don't get me wrong, the ingredients are so natural and wholesome that you absolutely could eat them, but you'll enjoy them much more in the bath. The calming fragrance of lavender will relax your mind, while the cocoa butter and coconut oil will melt and absorb into your skin, leaving it soft, smooth, and deeply hydrated. Just pop them into the hot water and soak for at least twenty minutes. These melts are a simple way to make any bath feel like a mini spa retreat—perfect for those days when you need a little extra self-care without any extra effort!

INGREDIENTS

- 55 grams (1.9 ounces) cocoa butter
- 25 grams (0.9 ounce) coconut oil
- 20 drops lavender essential oil
- 1 teaspoon dried lavender flowers

EQUIPMENT

- Kitchen scale
- Double boiler
- Silicone ice cube tray for mold

Treat Yourself with Cocoa Butter

Unrefined cocoa butter smells like a light, honeyed version of chocolate. It has intense hydrating properties and, when mixed with coconut oil, will seal moisture into the skin, leaving your whole body feeling and smelling wonderful.

1 Prepare and weigh the ingredients.

2 Melt the cocoa butter and coconut oil in a double boiler. Stir constantly and keep a watchful eye on the mixture. You want it to just reach the melting point and not overheat.

3 When the cocoa butter and coconut oil have melted and combined, add the essential oil and stir well. Immediately pour into a silicone mold.

4 Sprinkle the dried lavender buds on top of the hot oil, dividing them evenly between the bath melts.

5 Move the silicone mold to the refrigerator to cool for two hours until set. Store the finished bath melts in the fridge or a cool place if your house is warm.

After Bath Clean-Up

These bath melts are small, and much of the oil will absorb into your skin, but even so, some oil residue will remain on the sides of your tub. To clean up easily, use a kitchen scrubber with a handle that can be filled with soap. Fill the reservoir with the liquid hand soap from page 140 and give the sides of the tub a quick wash. Rinse with water and you are ready for your next bath.

Package a handful of these bath melts in a box lined with shredded parchment paper. Add a label on the outside of the box that says "Lavender Bath Melts" and a label on the inside that says "Add 1–2 melts per bath."

Coffee Bean Massage Bars

Makes four 50-gram (1.8-ounce) bars

Solid massage bars are a great way to soften skin without the mess of massage oil. The beeswax, cocoa butter, and coffee beans add so much fragrance to this recipe that no additional essential oils are needed for aroma. The soothing scent combination, skin-nourishing ingredients, and relaxation of a massage all come together for an at-home spa experience that will make weary muscles and minds feel renewed.

INGREDIENTS

- 65 grams (2.3 ounces) beeswax
- 65 grams (2.3 ounces) grapeseed oil
- 90 grams (3.2 ounces) cocoa butter
- 2 tablespoons roasted coffee beans

EQUIPMENT

- Kitchen scale
- Double boiler
- Oval silicone soap mold

Wake Up Tired Skin with Coffee

The coffee beans in these massage bars serve a dual purpose. First, those little round beans are the perfect shape to add a texture in the massage bar that feels great on your skin. Second, coffee antioxidants help calm inflamed skin. This makes for a massage bar that's both stimulating and calming at the same time.

1 Weigh the beeswax, grapeseed oil, and cocoa butter and add them to the top pot of a double boiler.

2 Divide the roasted coffee beans evenly between four of the cups in the silicone soap mold.

3 Heat the ingredients in the double boiler, stirring until they have all melted together.

4 Pour the ingredients into the silicone mold, dividing the contents equally.

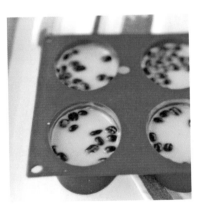

5 Leave the massage bars undisturbed until they are set. If you are making them in a warm room, move the silicone tray into the fridge to help them firm up.

6 Remove the bars from the mold and store them in the refrigerator when not in use.

Package a single massage bar in a burlap drawstring bag (which looks like a miniature burlap coffee sack!). Use letter stamps to create a label with the name of the bar. Give the edges of the label a burnished look by brushing them across an ink pad. A small grapevine heart attached to the tag and jute twine finishes off the wrapping.

Calendula Lotion Bars

Makes eight 57.5-gram (2-ounce) bars

Calendula (*Calendula officinalis*) is more than just a garden beauty—it also has a long-standing reputation as a natural anti-inflammatory skincare treatment. These lotion bars are made with grapeseed oil infused with calendula petals to give them a beautiful golden hue and all the delightful skin properties of calendula. The bars glide on your skin easily, are absorbed quickly, and don't leave you with a greasy feeling.

INGREDIENTS

- 200 grams (7.1 ounces) calendula-infused grapeseed oil
- 100 grams (3.5 ounces) virgin coconut oil
- 100 grams (3.5 ounces) beeswax
- 60 grams (2.1 ounces) cocoa butter
- A pinch of dried calendula petals (optional)
- 40 drops lavender essential oil (optional)

EQUIPMENT

- Kitchen scale
- Double boiler
- Silicone flower soap mold

The Healing Herb

Throughout history, calendula has been in ointments, salves, and poultices to treat burns, wounds, bruises, and inflammation of all kinds. Calendula speeds up the growth of tissue, which means it does wonders for healing minor cuts and scrapes quickly. It is also moisturizing and extremely gentle, so it is a good choice for children or those with sensitive skin.

1 Infuse the grapeseed oil with calendula petals as described on page 24.

2 Weigh the grapeseed oil, coconut oil, beeswax, and cocoa butter and add them to the top pot of a double boiler.

3 Heat the ingredients in the double boiler, stirring until they have all melted together.

4 If you're adding the lavender essential oil, stir it in now. Pour the ingredients into the silicone mold, dividing the contents equally. Sprinkle with calendula petals while still hot (optional).

5 Leave the lotion bars undisturbed until they are set. If you are making them in a warm room, move the silicone mold into the fridge to help them firm up.

6 Remove the bars from the mold and store them in the refrigerator when not in use.

Package up one lotion bar in a metal tin on a bed of shredded paper and calendula petals. Create a 2½"-diameter canning lid label and print it on craft paper. Use a 2½" hole punch to cut out the label as a perfectly round circle (or cut by hand). Add the label to the top of the tin. The loton bar is ready to gift!

Handcrafted
Lip Balm

Double Chocolate Mint Lip Balm

Makes six 4.5-milliliter (approximately 1-teaspoon) tubes

If you like chocolate as a dessert, you will love it in your lip balm! This lip balm has both cocoa butter and cocoa powder in it, giving it double the chocolatey skin benefits. Cocoa butter is ultra-moisturizing and readily absorbed into the skin because it melts at body temperature. Cocoa powder is rich in skin antioxidants and gives the lip balm a hint of color. The peppermint (*Mentha* x *piperita*) essential oil adds a cooling tingle to this luxurious lip balm and pairs perfectly with the chocolate.

INGREDIENTS

- 8 grams (0.3 ounce) coconut oil
- 8 grams (0.3 ounce) grapeseed oil
- 6 grams (0.2 ounce) castor oil
- 6 grams (0.2 ounce) beeswax
- 4 grams (0.15 ounce) cocoa butter
- ½ teaspoon organic cocoa powder
- 10 drops peppermint essential oil

MATERIALS

- Six 4.5-milliliter clear lip balm tubes

EQUIPMENT

- Kitchen scale
- Small double boiler with an inner pot that has a pour spout and handle

Mint Conditioning

In addition to adding a flavorful zing to the already delicious chocolate scent of this lip balm, mint essential oil tingles, cools, and invigorates lips while infusing them with vitamins that help to condition, repair, and protect dry, chapped skin.

1 Measure the coconut, grapeseed, and castor oil, along with the beeswax and cocoa butter, into a small double boiler. The top pot should be something with a handle and a pour spout so that it is easy to fill the lip balm tubes from the pot.

2 Put the double boiler on medium heat and stir the ingredients regularly until they are all melted together.

3 Take the pot off the heat and add the cocoa powder. Stir well with a small whisk. Add in the essential oil. Stir well with a small whisk.

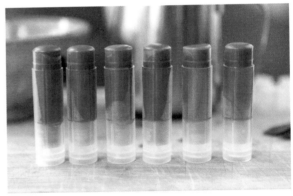

4 Twist each lip balm tube to be sure the risers are all set to the bottom. Carefully pour the lip balm into the tubes, filling each tube so the center screw is just covered. You should have some mixture left over.

5 Let the lip balm cool in the tubes, then warm up the remaining mixture in the pot and use it to top off each tube. Filling the tubes in two steps like this ensures you won't have a depressed top or a hole in the center of your lip balm. If this happens, add a little bit more mixture to the top of the depressed area and pass a flame over the top of the lip balm to melt the top smooth.

Create lip balm tube labels on the computer and print them on a sheet of colored craft label paper. The label size should be 1.69" x 2.125". When creating your designs, leave extra space at the top and bottom of each label, since these ends will overlap when wrapped around the tubes.

Honey Dandelion Lip Scrub

Makes one 30-gram (1-ounce) pot of scrub

Sure, you're familiar with dandelions (*Taraxacum officinale*), but have you ever smelled one? Their fragrance can range from an earthy smell to something quite sweet, but when the blossoms are picked at the right time, they have the aroma of honey. This isn't surprising, because they are one of the first food sources for bees each year. The flowers also make wonderful infused oil that is great for chapped lips. Paired with honey and sugar, this scrub makes lips very kissable.

INGREDIENTS

- 20 grams (0.7 ounce) sugar
- 5 grams (0.17 ounce) dandelion-infused olive oil
- 2 grams (0.07 ounce) honey

MATERIALS

- Small glass pot

EQUIPMENT

- Kitchen scale

Healing Honey

Honey has natural antibacterial properties and a ton of antioxidants that nourish and repair skin. It moisturizes, soothes, and stimulates tissue regeneration, making it a wonderful ingredient to relieve chapped, irritated lips.

1 Infuse olive oil with dandelion flowers following the instructions on page 24.

2 Lay out your ingredients.

3 Set a small dish on the kitchen scale and zero the scale. Add the sugar.

4 Zero the scale and add the honey and oil. Mix them together well. If you like the consistency, you can package it up now. If you would like it to be wetter, add more oil. If you would like it to be drier, add more sugar.

5 Spoon the mixture into a small glass pot. To use, apply a pea-sized amount to your lips and massage it in until the sugar has dissolved. Rinse with cool water and a cloth. Apply the lip balm of your choice (if desired). Store the scrub in a small, airtight container in the fridge for up to thirty days.

Foraging for Botanicals

The best botanicals are homegrown or purchased from reputable sources that have not treated them with any pesticides or herbicides. People are notorious for dousing dandelions in chemicals to remove them from their pristine lawns, so when foraging, look for dandelions in meadows or yards that you know have not been treated with chemical pesticides and herbicides. Those are not the ingredients you want to add to your skin!

Create a label on craft label paper and make a small tag with a bee stamp. Burnish the edges of the label and the tag by dragging them across a black ink pad. Attach the label to the top of the jar and attach the tag to the string of a small cotton muslin drawstring bag. Put the jar in the bag to deliver the lip scrub as a gift.

Peppermint Coconut Sugar Scrub

Makes one 400-gram (14.1-ounce) jar of scrub

Peppermint and coconut pair perfectly when it comes to brightening up your skin and your day. Mint has a cooling effect on the skin, and coconut oil is a powerful skin moisturizer. Plus, the fresh and tropical aroma will do wonders for your mood. This is a scrub that will make your skin smooth and soft, without the need to apply lotion after the shower.

INGREDIENTS

- 250 grams (8.8 ounces) sugar
- 125 grams (4.4 ounces) virgin coconut oil, softened
- 1 mint tea bag
- 10 drops peppermint essential oil
- Spirulina powder (optional)

MATERIALS

- Jar with lid

EQUIPMENT

- Kitchen scale

Deep Sea Greens

Spirulina is freshwater algae that heals skin and draws out toxins. Its deep green color adds a lot of personality to your home apothecary creations. Spirulina is also a popular superfood that is often added to green smoothies and supplements. Purchase it at a natural food store or a vitamin store in capsules, and use one or two when you want to color a recipe.

1 Lay out your ingredients. Set the coconut oil out in a warm place so that it softens but does not completely melt. Look for the consistency of softened butter as called for when baking.

2 In a bowl, cream together the sugar and the coconut oil.

3 Empty the contents of a tea bag into a small bowl. Sprinkle the herbs into the sugar scrub. You can add as much or as little as you would like, keeping in mind that adding more herbs can make the scrub more abrasive.

4 To give the scrub a minty green color, add in some spirulina powder as a natural colorant (optional).

5 Add the peppermint essential oil.

6 Stir the ingredients together and scoop into a lidded jar.

Tea Time!

The availability of herbal teas means there is an endless supply of dried herbs available to stock your home apothecary. Simply break open a bag of organic herbal or green tea and use the dried herbs inside as an addition to your favorite plant-based beauty recipes.

Package the scrub in a jar with a chalkboard label, then use a liquid chalk pen to write the name of the scrub. Wrap jute twine around the top of the jar, just under the lid, and tie in a bow.

Healing Himalayan Pink Salt Scrub

Makes one 250-gram (8.8-ounce) jar of scrub

Don't let the pretty pink color of this scrub fool you into thinking it's all shine with no substance. The salt exfoliates and smoothes skin, while nourishing minerals penetrate skin to heal, detoxify, and rejuvenate. The rose petals and fragrant essential oil make this recipe healing and calming for both body and mind. All that and pink too? What's not to love?

INGREDIENTS

- 200 grams (7.1 ounces) pink Himalayan sea salt
- 50 grams (1.8 ounces) coconut oil
- 25 grams (0.9 ounce) rose-infused sweet almond oil
- 8 drops rose geranium essential oil
- Dried rose petals (optional)

MATERIALS

- Small, airtight container

EQUIPMENT

- Kitchen scale

In the Pink

The pretty pink color of Himalayan salt is more than just pleasing to the eye—it is caused by iron and other minerals in the salt. The beneficial minerals are easily absorbed through the skin and help to heal damaged muscle tissue. The minerals also work to draw out impurities and detoxify while you soak, so you just might come out of the bath feeling like a new person.

1 Infuse sweet almond oil with rose petals following the instructions on page 24.

2 Lay out your ingredients. Set the coconut oil out in a warm place so that it softens but does not completely melt. Look for the consistency of softened butter as called for when baking.

3 Weigh the sea salt and coconut oil on a kitchen scale.

4 Mix the sea salt, infused almond oil, and coconut oil together well. If you would like it to be wetter, add more oil. If you would like it to be drier, add more salt. When you are happy with the consistency, add the essential oil and stir to combine.

5 Top with dried rose petals (optional) and store in a small, airtight container in the fridge for up to thirty days.

Scrub Up!

This Himalayan pink salt scrub is best when applied before a warm bath. Massage into wet skin all over the body and soak in a warm bath for at least twenty minutes. Rest, relax, and dry your skin thoroughly after the bath. Bring a cool glass of water to the bath with you, since detoxification can be powerful.

You may feel a bit woozy right afterward. Drink at least two 8-ounce glasses of water during and within an hour after the bath. If this routine is being done before bed, you should have a wonderful night's rest.

Add a piece of lace over the top of the scrub and secure it with the lid. Tie a ribbon around the edge of the lid. A handwritten or printed label finishes off the look.

Aromatherapy Perfume

Makes one 10-milliliter (approximately 2-teaspoon) aromatherapy perfume

Roller bottles are popular in aromatherapy as a way to apply an individual dose of herbal benefits for a variety of different moods and ailments. Roller bottles can also make beautiful perfume bottles. By replacing lab-created fragrances with naturally occurring essential oils, you'll not only smell good, you'll feel pretty good too.

Blending essential oils is a skill that takes practice. To get started, take a few of the scents you are usually drawn to and hold the open bottles to your nose. When you breathe in the combination of fragrances, you'll learn what you like and what you don't.

When you find a combination you like, spend some time blending the oils together using different ratios to come up with a fragrance that works for you. For the strongest-scented oils, start with only one drop and add more if it's not strong enough. There are some scents—like lemongrass and cinnamon—that are so strong they can take over the entire blend.

INGREDIENTS

- 9 milliliters carrier oil of your choice
- 10 drops essential oil blend
- Fresh and dried flowers and herbs

MATERIALS

- One 10-milliliter glass roll-on bottle

Understanding Notes

The fragrance characteristics of essential oils are classified as "notes"—specifically, top notes, middle notes, and base notes. Top notes are light, fresh, and fast-acting, and they tend to evaporate very quickly. This is usually the first scent you smell in a blend. Middle notes help to balance the blend. You might not smell the middle note right away, but the soft fragrance may become apparent after a few minutes. Base notes are very strong and heavy, grounding the blend with their long-lasting diffusion. Balance your perfume creations by blending different notes together to make the end result complex and alluring. Here are some examples.

- *TOP NOTES: bergamot, lemongrass, grapefruit, orange, geranium, peppermint, eucalyptus*
- *MIDDLE NOTES: lavender, rose, mandarin orange, cypress, cinnamon bark*
- *BASE NOTES: patchouli, cedarwood, sandalwood, frankincense, ginger*

1 Spend some time blending essential oils to come up with a fragrance that works for you. Collect fresh or dried petals and leaves to use in the bottle. Prepare the roller bottle by removing the lid and roller ball.

2 Fill the bottle with the carrier oil. Choose fractionated coconut oil if you don't want your perfume to have any color. Other oils (such as grapeseed oil, sweet almond oil, or jojoba oil) will be in various shades of amber and green (grapeseed oil is shown here).

3 Add 10 drops of your essential oil blend to the bottle.

4 Add a combination of fresh and dried flowers, leaves, or petals into the oil to decorate the bottle.

5 Pop the roller ball lid onto the glass vial. Shake well to combine the oils.

6 Leave the blend for twenty-four to forty-eight hours to develop. As the oils work together, the scent will change. You may be surprised at how different it is when it's done!

Carrier Oils

Carrier oils are oils used to suspend and deliver essential oils. They are the base that you add essential oils to so they are properly diluted before being applied to your skin. Good choices for carrier oils are thin oils without a strong fragrance. Choose fractionated coconut oil, grapeseed oil, sweet almond oil, or jojoba oil to make aromatherapy perfume.

*Package up a collection of four different scents in a craft paper jewelry box.
Use washi tape with a message to create a band on the box lid.*

Botanical Bath Time

Are you a bath or shower person? I was a shower person for so long so that I could efficiently get ready to run off to whatever was next on my jam-packed schedule. Then I found something wonderful that made a huge difference in my overall well-being: a bath. It sounds so simple, doesn't it? If you have access to a bathtub, I encourage you to replace at least one shower per week with an herbal bath. Soaking in warm water, salts, and botanicals is pain relieving, detoxifying, and relaxing. It's like pushing a reset button on your day. I swear by a bath after a long day on my feet or in the garden to soothe aches and pains and relieve tension. And bathing just before bed will help you drift off into dreamland utterly relaxed.

Tips for Bath Time

Light a candle to set the mood. Fill the tub with warm water, add some bath salts or a bath bomb made from the recipes in this book, and consider tossing in some flower petals from the garden. Drink a big glass of water while you soak and put away your phone or tablet. Just breathe the aromas and let the warm water work its magic.

Creative Candles

When I began candle making,

I was pleasantly surprised at how easy it was to make artisanal creations. Having the opportunity to make something handmade allows you to play and unleash your creativity. It's time well spent, and you will be gobsmacked by your gorgeous creations! These lovely recipes will give you a treasure trove of great gifts, plus they are fun to make with friends and family.

In this book, candles are the least consumable type of product, in that they don't nourish your skin or body or clean your home—but they are essential in their own way as both a creative outlet and a daily reminder to slow down and enjoy the small moments. The air you breathe in your home can still have an impact on your health and mood—hence the recipes in this section, which feature natural ingredients that burn cleanly and thoughtful scents that can help set the stage for your self-care.

The recipes presented here will suit many different occasions and seasons, from scenting a relaxing night at home, to adding some seasonal cheer in winter, to brightening and energizing a stuffy room. With just wax, wicks, and fragrance, there is no reason why even a beginner can't handcraft magnificent projects right in their kitchen.

Getting Started

There are many different types of candles: container candles, votives, pillars, tapers, and more. Some techniques require years of practice and special equipment, but there are also candles that are simple to make at home, and that's what this book focuses on. In this section, you'll learn a number of techniques for how to make container candles and wax melts, using equipment and supplies that are readily available at craft stores and online. I'll cover candle safety, equipment and ingredients, and some invaluable tips and troubleshooting. Once you understand the basics, you will be able to make any of the projects in this book, as well as fire up your own creative ideas to combine containers and scents in different ways.

About Candles

CONTAINER CANDLES

Making container candles allows for a great deal of creativity because you can customize so many parts of the process: melting wax, adding color and fragrance, pouring it into a heatproof container, and adding a wick. If a container is in the appropriate shape to hold a candle, and it is made of a material that can withstand the heat of molten wax, then you can probably make a candle in it! A few other considerations like volume and shape will help you to make the best container candle.

CONTAINER VOLUME: A candle can be made in a small container or a large container—you will simply need to adjust the amount of wax and number of wicks needed. A small candle is a wonderful use of expensive materials like beeswax and essential oils, while a large candle will require a lot more materials. Large candles will also need multiple wicks to burn the candle to the edges.

CONTAINER SHAPE: Flames need oxygen, so the container should have a wide opening to allow for proper air exposure. Containers that widen below the neck of a smaller opening may not burn evenly and can produce excessive smoke.

WAX MELTS

A wax melt is a scented, shaped piece of wax that can be melted in an electric- or candle-heated ceramic warmer to release the scent. Wax melts are a way to get all of the fragrance and warmth of a candle without the flame. The beauty of wax melts is that you can use botanicals and dry herbs to decorate your projects without the worry of them catching fire. The electric options also keep your home safe from flames if you have young children or pets.

CANDLE SAFETY

Candles are a wonderful way to add natural light and fragrance, but they are also no joke when it comes to fire safety. Candles should never be burned unattended. Keep them out of the path of children and pets and never add things near the flame like glitter or herbs that can spark and float into the air. Be prepared to extinguish the candle by covering it with a candle snuffer. Do not throw water on a candle to extinguish it, and don't touch the melted wax or move the candle with melted wax while it is still liquid, to prevent splatters, spills, and burns. Always use your common sense with any DIY project, especially when fire is involved.

Equipment

Wax, dyes, and scent oils are difficult to remove completely from pots and jars, so set aside a stash of equipment just for candle making. Many of the tools that you need for candle making can be easily found in your kitchen or craft drawer. Luckily, these items are also very easy to acquire at thrift and department stores, allowing you to dedicate the equipment to the craft.

DOUBLE BOILER

A double boiler is the safest way to melt wax without burning it; however, you don't need to have a proper double boiler for candle making. You can make your own using two pots, one for water and one for wax. It's nice to use a candle-making pitcher as the wax pot, because it has a pour spout that allows for accuracy when pouring. You can also make a small double boiler by using a pot or pan and a heatproof container like a glass canning jar or glass measuring cup.

CANDLE-MAKING PITCHER OR OTHER HEATPROOF CONTAINER

A heatproof container with a pour spout in metal or glass is very helpful when making candles. This can be a large, aluminum candle-making pitcher for making a bunch of candles at a time or a glass measuring cup for making wax melts or individual candles.

KITCHEN UTENSILS

A long-handled wooden spoon works well to stir the wax in a tall pot, a regular soup spoon works just fine for stirring a smaller pot, and a ladle makes pouring the candles more precise when you have a large pot of wax.

THERMOMETER

A candle-making thermometer with a clip to hold on to the side of a candle-making pitcher will allow you to know when your wax is at the perfect temperature for pouring, adding color, and adding scent.

KITCHEN SCALE

A kitchen scale is required for weighing the wax and scent oil to be sure that you have the right mix. It is fine to either follow the metric quantities given (grams and milliliters) or the US quantities given (ounces). Note that ounces are always indicating standard ounces, not fluid ounces, even when measuring a liquid—so use the same kitchen scale and method to measure all ounce quantities. Don't risk the imprecision of trying to convert non-volumetric measurements, like grams or ounces, to volumetric measurements instead.

PAPER CUPS OR SHOT GLASSES

A set of recyclable mini paper cups or shot glasses are perfect for measuring scent oils and for premixing solid wax dye chips.

HOT GLUE GUN OR WAX ADHESIVE

A hot glue gun, with hot glue sticks, is a useful tool for affixing the wick to the bottom of a container before pouring the wax. You can also purchase a special wax adhesive for the same purpose.

CHOPSTICKS OR WOODEN CLOTHESPINS

Once your candles are poured, clothespins and chopsticks will help to keep the wick centered properly as the candle cools.

Materials

There are only a few materials that you need to make a candle: wax, a wick, and, optionally, dye and essential oil. Within each of those, there are a few things to consider.

WAX

SOY WAX: Soy wax is a vegetable-based wax that is a hydrogenated form of soybean oil. It has a creamy white color, a lower melting point, and longer burning time than paraffin wax. Some brands of soy wax can create dimples when burned, giving the candle a less attractive appearance than paraffin candles. It can be purchased as a solid or flake form. Solid is often more economical, while flakes are easier to melt.

BEESWAX: Raw, unfiltered beeswax, created by honeybees, can have a lovely honey scent. Beeswax can be more expensive, but it doesn't need fragrance added. Processed beeswax will have a lighter color and lighter scent and is available in variations of gold and white. It is available in bricks or small pellets called pastilles. Bricks can be more economical, while pastilles are easier to melt.

PARAFFIN WAX: This kind of wax burns very well and has been used for more than 150 years to make candles, but I recommend soy wax or beeswax over it. It is a byproduct of crude oil and is the least eco-friendly option for candle making, but if you have old candles made from paraffin wax, they can be recycled into making some of the projects in this book. Paraffin wax can be purchased in blocks, pellets, and sand form. Blocks are often more economical, while pellets are easier to melt.

Different waxes can be blended to gain the benefits of each of the ingredients. Blend paraffin and soy wax to improve the consistency of the wax texture when burned and to prevent dimpling. Blend beeswax and soy wax to get a subtle version of the color of beeswax and the sweet honey aroma at a more affordable price. Feel free to experiment with blending or purchase premade wax blends.

DYE

WAX DYE: This kind of dye, which comes in solid and liquid forms, is specifically formulated for candle making and will give you the most even color and burn performance. Liquid wax dye is the easiest dye to use because it doesn't need to be dissolved like solid dye does. Solid wax dye comes in blocks or chips that can be dissolved into melted wax to obtain the desired color.

CRAYONS: These are inexpensive, readily available, and come in every color of the rainbow. Crayons are full of dye and are made from wax, so they are often used to add color to candle projects, but there are some warnings to this as well. They could add some undesirable characteristics to your candles, like a clogged wick or a crayon smell when burned. To avoid this, only use crayons in very small amounts to give a hint of color to a project. Also test burn one candle before making a large number of them.

WICKS

Wicks come in many different materials and forms, from basic cotton on a roll to wired and waxed wicks with tabs (see more detail at right). No matter which you choose, you need the right size (thickness) for your candle to burn properly. Wicks that are too small will not melt the wax all the way to the edge of the candle, creating a tunnel in the center. Wicks that are too large will create a lot of smoke. (However, both of the aforementioned situations are also used as techniques in projects in this book—there's an exception to every rule!) Look for labeling on the package of wicks to see what wax and candle diameter they are appropriate for.

Keep wicks trimmed to ⅛" to ¼" for best results. Be sure to only trim the wicks once the candles have fully cooled and cured for twenty-four hours.

Wick Types

- *Cotton wicks* come as a roll of cotton string that has been braided to provide thickness. HTP™ wicks are a specific kind of cotton wick that I recommend for several of the candle projects.

- *Wired wicks* have a thin zinc wire in the center that helps to hold the wick straight.

- *Waxed wicks* are coated with wax. If you are making a paraffin candle, use a paraffin-coated wick. If you are making a soy or beeswax candle, use a soy wax–coated wick (a soy wax–coated wick has proven to perform better than a beeswax-coated wick in a beeswax candle).

- *Wood wicks* are flat wicks made of soft wood that sound like a crackling fire when they burn. Wood wicks do not need trimming after they are burned.

Tabs—not a kind of wick, but an element of some wicks—are metal disks (or, in the case of wood wicks, metal rectangles) that weigh the wick down and give you a place to glue the wick to the bottom of the container.

Candle-Making Temperature

Color and scent are added at a higher temperature than you will pour the candle at. The temperature differs depending on what type of wax you are using, since different waxes have differing melting points. Soy wax will melt at somewhere between 120ºF and 180ºF depending on the blend. The packaging or instructions should list both the temperature to add color and scent as well as the temperature to pour the wax. For example, using a basic container blend of soy wax flakes, you would add the fragrance and color when the wax reaches 160ºF and stir thoroughly for one minute. Then cool the wax to a lower temperature, between 140ºF and 150ºF, to pour it. Adding the scent oil and dye at the right time ensures that it will properly bind to the wax and be evenly distributed. Pouring at the right temperature ensures you will have the best-looking candles by preventing a host of problems.

SCENT

Candle scent is differentiated by hot throw (the scent that a candle gives off when burned) and cold throw (the scent that an unlit candle gives off). I use essential oils to scent all of my candles, because, like so many others, I have sensitivities to synthetic fragrance oils.

ESSENTIAL OILS: These are natural scents extracted from plants and are often better tolerated by people with scent sensitivities or allergies. Even so, some folks are sensitive to concentrated scents, so use scents sparingly and keep an eye out for reactions. There are many wonderful benefits to scenting candles with essential oils, though. They fill our spaces with heavenly aromas that can have different healing effects (such as relaxation or focus). They typically have expected cold throw, but they can be inconsistent with hot throw, since each oil type and oil manufacturer will produce oils with differing qualities. When we make candles with essential oils, we add in the scent at the very end and pour the candles quickly, minimizing evaporation. Ask at your local candle-making shop for essential oils that are formulated for candle making. If you can't find them, never fear, because normal essential oils do work well in candles if you follow the steps in this chapter. Depending on the scent you choose, they may result in a milder scent, which is not necessarily a bad thing—a little aromatherapy goes a long way.

FRAGRANCE OILS: Most candle stores sell fragrance oil (artificial fragrance) even though many people are sensitive to them. This is because fragrance oils offer the most consistent and reliable scent. They have been formulated to be heated to high temperatures and added to molten wax without evaporation. Fragrance oils also come in a wide variety of lab-created scents like mango and green apple that are pleasing and not available as essential oils. When you walk into a candle-making store, you will see that the fragrances are cheaper and have a much wider range. As tempting as they may be, many people have concerns with toxicity or reactions. I encourage you to lean into the power of our plant allies and bypass the "strawberry cheesecake" fragrance.

Fragrance load is how much scent oil the wax will hold. A common fragrance load for soy wax is 1 ounce of scent oil per 1 pound of wax, or a 6.25% ratio. You can increase or decrease the ratio depending on how strong the scent is to ensure that the scent neither disappears nor overpowers. For subtly fragrant oils, increase the ratio to 8%–10%; for strongly scented oils, reduce the ratio to 6%–8%.

When you are starting out, using the 1-ounce-per-pound-of-wax rule is both easy to measure and a safe bet that the candle will turn out well. With more than a 7% fragrance load, some candles can have issues with wicking. Be sure to check the maximum on the wax you are using if you plan to go higher.

To calculate how much scent oil is needed for any given quantity of wax, use this formula: (oz. of wax) x (% scent oil) = (oz. of scent oil needed).

Basic Process

The projects in this book show many methods of crafting candles in different styles, but the basic steps for making container candles and wax melts are generally the same, no matter what wax, wicks, or containers you use. Follow these basic steps to make a simple container candle, then visit the projects to get ideas for how to craft and style something personal and creative.

1. Select an appropriate container for your candle. Any heatproof container that is clean and free from cracks or holes is a good choice. Some potential options are glass canning jars, glass candle holders, metal tins, ceramic tea or coffee cups, and seashells.

2. If required, assemble the wick so that it has a metal tab on the bottom. For a cotton wick, thread it through the hole in the metal tab and clamp the hole shut using pliers. Trim the excess wick from the bottom of the tab so that it sits flat in the bottom of the container.

3. Add the wick to the container with a dab of hot glue or wax adhesive on the bottom of the tab. Press it firmly to the bottom center of the container. If you can't reach your fingers into the container, use a straw or a pen casing with the ink removed to press it down firmly.

4. Assemble a double boiler by filling the bottom pot with a few inches of water and reserving the inner pot for melting the wax.

5. Weigh the required amount of wax on a kitchen scale by zeroing the scale with the inner part of the double boiler on the scale and then adding the wax. If using wax blocks, cut them into smaller pieces before melting.

6. Weigh the required amount of fragrance or essential oil using a kitchen scale. Small paper cups or shot glasses make a perfect tool for this! Set the fragrance or essential oil aside.

7. Heat the wax over medium heat until the wax is completely melted and reaches the temperature indicated in the recipe or on the packaging from the wax you have purchased.

8. If you are adding color and scent, bring the temperature up to the temperature specified on the wax packaging (for example, 160°F) for adding dye and scent oil (see "Candle-Making Temperature" on page 84).

9. Remove the wax from the heat and stir the dye in until it is completely dissolved. The amount of dye you need per pound of wax will be listed on the package of wax dye, or you can blend until you like the hue, keeping in mind that it will change when the candle is dry. To determine the final wax color, place a spoonful of wax in a paper cup of cold water. It will dry quickly, and you will see the final color when you remove the wax from the water.

Tips, Tricks, and Troubleshooting

In candle making, there are a few issues that might arise with the appearance, burning, or scent of your candle projects. This list of tips and tricks can help to troubleshoot any problems you may run into.

- In many cases, pouring container candles in two steps is not necessary, but it can also depend on the wax you use and varying room and wax temperature. If you get a depressed area around the wick when cooled, warm up some more wax and pour a thin layer of wax on top of the candle to smooth out the surface.

- You can also smooth out the top surface of a candle by using a low-temperature heat gun. Do not try using a blow dryer, since it will melt and splatter the wax.

- Some brands of soy wax can create dimples when burned, giving the candle a less attractive appearance. If this happens, consider using a soy wax blend or using a different brand of soy wax.

- Cracks in a candle can happen if the wax was cooled too quickly or left in a cold room.

- Use a soft cloth to buff the surface of your candle to give it a smooth appearance.

- Heat the container on a candle-warming pad before pouring the candle, and cool it slowly to prevent "wet spots."

- Use the right-sized wick and keep it trimmed to ¼" long to avoid excess smokiness.

- If the wick disappears into the pool of wax, the wick diameter may be too small for the candle. Use a larger-diameter wick next time.

- The right size wick is one that will allow the candle wax to burn all the way to the edges without being too large (which would cause the candle to smoke). Test a different size wick to see if that improves your results.

- If the candle scent isn't as strong as you would like it, use a reliable essential oil created for candle making. Adding more essential oil than the recipe calls for may end up being too much oil for the wax to bind with, leaving you with excess oil at the surface and bottom of the candle.

- Pour leftover wax into a silicone cupcake or soap mold to cool. The puck-shaped wax will be easy to melt the next time you want to make candles.

- Wipe wax from containers and utensils using a paper towel while the wax is still warm. Once the wax sets, it is much more difficult to clean off the equipment. Do not pour wax down the drain.

- When adding anything into a candle other than wax, wicks, scent oils, and dyes made for candle making, be aware that it could catch on fire. If you add herbs or other elements like glitter, color, or even essential oils to a candle, they can react in a way that you might not expect.

Warning

Never burn a candle unless you remain in attendance. Always be prepared to extinguish a candle by covering it. Do not throw water on a burning candle, since it can cause the wax to splatter.

Warming Cappuccino Candle

Makes one 225-gram (8-ounce) candle

It's likely that you have a few unused coffee cups lying around the house. There are so many stylish coffee cups out there, it's easy to buy one every time you visit a store. Before you know it, you have more mugs than you know what to do with. Here is what to do with them: make a candle! These cinnamon-scented candles have an invigorating (and yummy) aroma and are yet another way for a coffee cup lover to enjoy waking up.

INGREDIENTS

- 225 grams (8 ounces) soy wax for container candles
- 24 milliliters (0.8 ounce) cinnamon essential oil

MATERIALS

- One 4" bowl-shaped coffee cup with a wide mouth
- One wood wick and metal tab

EQUIPMENT

- Double boiler
- Hot glue gun and glue or wax adhesive
- Thermometer
- Old towel
- Fine-tip pruning shears
- Kitchen scale
- Paper cup
- Heatproof container with pour spout

Tip: Customize the color of the candle to match your favorite coffee. Leave the soy wax natural to match the white foam of a cappuccino or add brown wax dye to change the color of the candle to the warm tone of coffee with cream.

Wake Up & Smell the Coffee

Research shows that it's not just the caffeine in coffee that wakes you up—the aroma of coffee also has the power to add cheer and energy to your day. So, if you are trying to kick the caffeine habit, or just want a little extra pep in your step, add some coffee beans to the top of this candle just as the wax begins to harden. Use a chopstick to guide them to the edges; as the wax warms, the beans will also warm and release the coffee aroma.

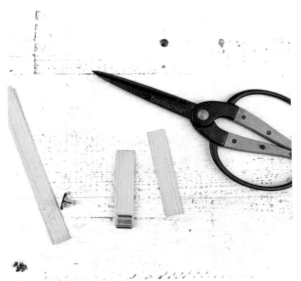

1 Weigh the soy wax and add it to a double boiler on medium heat. While the wax is melting, measure the scent oil into a paper cup.

2 Prepare the wood wick by measuring the final height in the cup, ¼" above the final top of the wax; cut the wick. Feed the wooden wick into the metal base and use a dab of hot glue or wax adhesive to attach it to the bottom of the cup at the center.

3 When the melted wax has reached the specified temperature for adding dye or scent oil (for example, 160°F—see the instructions that came with your wax), add the scent oil and wax dye (if using). Stir well to bind.

4 Cool the wax to 140°F and pour it into the cup. Wrap the candle in a towel and place it in a warm room to slowly set.

5 Allow your candle to cure for forty-eight hours undisturbed. Once cured, trim the wick with fine-tip pruning shears if it is more than ¼" above the wax.

Pair the candle up with a bag of gourmet roasted coffee beans or a gift card to a favorite café for a coffee-themed gift. Add a cute tag that reads "I like you a latte," "Thanks a latte," or "Words can't espresso my love for you."

Clay Pot Citronella Candles

Makes three 2½" clay pot candles

Nothing ruins a summer party more quickly than unwanted guests like mosquitoes and other biting insects! These clay pot candles not only keep pests away but also make great summer table decorations.

INGREDIENTS

- 450 grams (16 ounces) soy wax for container candles
- 30 milliliters (1 ounce) pure citronella oil (also called citronella essential oil)

MATERIALS

- Three 2½"-diameter terra-cotta pots
- Electrical tape
- Silicone sealer
- Cork sheet
- Three 6" large to extra-large waxed and wired wicks with tabs (such as HTP-1312)
- Water-based, nonflammable sealer, such as Mod Podge®
- Disposable foam paintbrush

EQUIPMENT

- Hot glue gun and glue
- Double boiler
- Metal tray
- Old towel
- Thermometer
- Sharp scissors
- Kitchen scale
- Paper cup
- Chopsticks or clothespins
- Heatproof container with pour spout

Bug Off, Naturally

The citronella scent sends annoying bugs flying in the opposite direction, so these pretty candles are perfect additions to your outdoor table for summer evenings on the patio that you want to enjoy itch free. The common misconception is that mosquitoes are repelled by the smell, but that's not correct. In fact, the scent helps to mask your scent. As the candles burn, they release the oil into the air, effectively hiding you from mosquitoes. Ah, the power of nature. Citronella candles are meant to add ambiance and some comfort to your outdoor spaces, not to protect you from Zika, malaria, or other mosquito-borne illnesses. If you live somewhere where those diseases are heavily present, or if you are higher risk, use common sense and get protection. That being said, if you are out in your garden or on your patio having a glass of wine, and you put a few of these candles around to protect your space, they can be really effective!

1 Use a foam brush to apply the water-based sealer to the inside of each pot. Seal up the hole of each pot by placing a few pieces of electrical tape inside the pot, covering the hole.

2 Flip each pot over and fill the hole with silicone sealer. Cut a cork sheet circle that will fit inside the bottom rim of the pot. Use a hot glue gun to attach the cork to the bottom of the pot once the silicone has completely dried.

3 Melt 1 pound of soy wax flakes in a double boiler and add a thermometer. While the wax is melting, measure the citronella oil into a paper cup and attach a wick to the inner bottom of each clay pot using hot glue.

4 When the melted wax has reached the specified temperature for adding dye or scent oil (for example, 160°F—see the instructions that came with your wax), add the citronella oil. Stir well for a full minute to make sure that the oil is completely mixed into the wax.

5 Set the clay pots on a metal tray to protect your work surface from spills or leaks. Use chopsticks or clothespins to keep the wick upright and straight. Cool the wax to 140°F and pour into each of the pots to ½" from the top.

6 Wrap the candles in a towel and allow to dry completely untouched in a warm room. Allow your candles to cure for forty-eight hours undisturbed. When the candles are cured, trim the wicks to ¼" above the wax.

A set of three citronella candles placed in a chicken wire basket has the right feel for the outdoors. Paint the pots with water-based acrylic paint, add a topcoat of sealer, and tie cords around the rims to jazz up the candles. If you want to give them as a gift, a checkered towel, burlap ribbon, and stamped tag make for a pretty presentation.

Tip: The right size wick will burn a candle all the way to the edges of the container without creating a lot of extra smoke. Using a wick that is considered too large for the container increases the amount of smoke the candle produces. Because these candles are meant to be burned outdoors, choose a larger wick than would normally be appropriate.

Citrus Celebration Wax Melts

Makes twelve 15-gram (0.5-ounce) wax melts

The festive scent of these citrus wax melts is both cheerful and uplifting and will give any home a refreshing, energizing feel. An ice cube mold is the perfect size for these melts, which are topped with lemon, lime, and orange zest. You will want to make enough for yourself and all your friends! If you want to gift these to someone who doesn't have a wax warmer, package together a pretty wax warmer along with a batch of the melts.

INGREDIENTS

- 170 grams (6 ounces) soy wax for wax melts
- 12 milliliters (0.4 ounce) citrus blend essential oils
- One each: fresh lemon, lime, and orange
- Wax dye (optional)

EQUIPMENT

- Double boiler
- Thermometer
- Kitchen scale
- Paper cup
- Heatproof container with a pour spout
- Citrus zester
- Silicone ice cube tray

Celebrate with Citrus!

The bright and cheery aroma of citrus is fresh and lively, but also very calming. Use citrus-scented candles and wax melts to make your home smell fresh, clean, and welcoming. But don't use a grapefruit scent before a dinner party, because it is said to curb the appetite!

1 Weigh the soy wax and scent oil.

2 Set up a small double boiler using a heatproof glass jar to hold the wax and a metal bread pan filled partway with water. Stir the wax frequently until it is fully melted.

3 Use the zester to grate the three fruits. Mix the zest together.

4 Bring the wax to the specified temperature for adding dye or scent oil (for example, 160°F—see the instructions that came with your wax). Add in scent and color (if using) and stir until completely mixed.

5 If you heated the wax in a canning jar, transfer it to a heatproof container with a pour spout for more accuracy when pouring it into the molds. Pour the wax into a silicone ice cube tray and immediately sprinkle the citrus zest on top of each melt.

6 Allow the wax melts to dry completely before popping them out of the mold for use. To use, add one or two wax melts to an electric or tea light wax warmer and enjoy the fragrance.

For a great gift, fill a small canning jar with citrus wax melts and pair it with a tea light wax warmer. Stack and wrap the jar and the wax warmer with a tea light candle, all tied together with a natural ribbon.

Herbal Sleepy Time Wax Melts

Makes twenty-five 9-gram (0.3-ounce) wax melts

With busy days and hectic schedules, we could all use a good night's sleep. These herbal chamomile (*Matricaria chamomilla*), calendula, and lavender wax melts are the perfect way to send you to dreamland, as the calming scent of herbs will fill the room and relax you as the wax melts. Pull them out whenever you are in need of a restful evening.

INGREDIENTS

- 225 grams (8 ounces) microwaveable soy wax for wax melts
- 10 milliliters (0.34 ounce) lavender essential oil
- 5 milliliters (0.17 ounce) orange essential oil
- 1 tablespoon each: dried lavender buds, chamomile flowers, and calendula petals

EQUIPMENT

- Heatproof container with a pour spout
- Microwave
- Kitchen scale
- Paper cup
- Silicone candy/baking/soap mold in a flower shape

Sleepy Time Herb Blend

There are some herbs that wake you up and others that quiet you down. Herbs like lavender, chamomile, calendula, hops, mint, and passionflower are calming for the nerves and quieting for the mind. Using these herbs before bed can help to promote an easier time falling asleep as well as better quality of sleep.

Making this recipe as herbal wax melts instead of a candle allows the wax, oils, and herbs to melt together at a safe temperature without risk that the herbs will catch fire. Of course, never leave a candle burning at bedtime.

This recipe can be made in either a microwave or in a double boiler. The steps to make wax melts in the microwave are outlined here. To make this recipe in a double boiler, use the same materials but follow the instructions and use the equipment in the Citrus Celebration Wax Melts project (see page 97).

1 Weigh microwaveable soy wax for wax melts in a heatproof container with a pour spout.

2 Weigh scent oil in a paper cup. Prepare the herbs in advance of using the microwave so you are ready to add them as soon as the wax has melted.

3 Melt the wax in twenty-second intervals to be sure it melts and doesn't cook. You may be tempted to set the timer for longer than twenty seconds, since you will see little change in the wax at first. After a few intervals, you will see the wax quickly turn from a solid to a liquid. Overheating the wax can cause it to burn and smell terrible, so set twenty-second intervals and check the wax frequently.

4 When the wax has fully melted, stir in the scent oil and half of the dried herbs.

5 Pour the wax into a flower-shaped mold. Choose a mold used for soapmaking or candy making to be sure it can handle the heat of the melted wax.

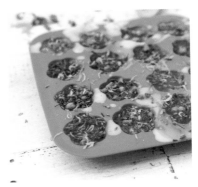

6 Sprinkle the remaining herbs on top of each melt and allow the herbal wax melts to dry completely before popping them out.

To store and display (or gift!) your melts, fill a wax-lined window bag with the melts and label the bag with letter stamps. Use floral stamps to further embellish the sack. Move the melts around inside the bag so their pretty faces show through the window.

Healing Crystals Candle

Makes one 4" tin candle

These healing candles are like a secret treasure. The silver tin is what you would expect to hold a candle, but once you open up the tin, you're greeted with a pretty pink, fragrant candle topped with glittering crystals. There are three wicks in this candle, which allows the wide surface to burn evenly.

INGREDIENTS

- 140 grams (5 ounces) soy wax for container candles
- 9 milliliters (0.3 ounce) essential oils blend containing lavender, lemongrass, mandarin orange, patchouli, geranium, and ylang-ylang
- 1" piece of pink crayon

MATERIALS

- One 4" tin container with lid
- Three 2½" large waxed and wired wicks with tabs (such as HTP-104)
- Assorted crystals

EQUIPMENT

- Double boiler
- Hot glue gun and glue or wax adhesive
- Thermometer
- Sharp scissors
- Kitchen scale
- Paper cup
- Heatproof container with pour spout

Healing Crystals

The crystals used in this project are decorative, but if you want to add a special element to this candle, visit a crystal shop and find some healing crystals. Some ideas could be stones associated with relaxation (amethyst), healing (quartz), luck (jade), and success (citrine).

1 Measure and melt the soy wax in a double boiler with a thermometer. While the wax is melting, measure the scent oil into a paper cup.

2 Place the wicks at half the radius of the container, evenly spaced at three points around the base of the candle as if there were three candles set together inside the tin. Attach each of the wicks with wax adhesive or hot glue.

3 When the melted wax has reached the specified temperature for adding dye or scent oil (for example, 160°F— see the instructions that came with your wax), add in 1" of pink crayon cut into pieces. Stir well until the color has completely dissolved into the wax.

4 If the wax has cooled, put it back on the heat to bring it up to temperature and add the scent oil. Stir well to ensure the oil is completely mixed into the wax.

5 Cool the wax to 140°F and pour it into the tin around the wicks, leaving ¼" of headspace. The headspace will allow the tin to close even with the crystals in place.

6 Leave the candle untouched to set just enough so that the crystals will not slip down into the wax. The wax should still be slightly warm to the touch; gently press each crystal on the wax surface so that it attaches to the wax. Be careful not to press the crystals too hard, since this can create cracks in the wax surface. Trim the wicks to ¼".

The fun of this candle is the secret treasure that is hidden within a silver tin embellished with gold gem stickers. Buy sheets of stickers and customize the pattern for a one-of-a-kind treasure.

Jam Jar Candle Favors

Makes twelve 100-gram (3.5-ounce) candles

These jam jar candles make beautiful, natural gifts, and they're easier to make than you think. They're so easy that you can produce a lot in a short period of time, making them perfect for wedding favors, a shower gift, or a handmade candle-making bonanza!

INGREDIENTS

- 1.2 kilograms (2 pounds and 10 ounces) soy wax for container candles
- 75 milliliters (2.6 ounces) your choice essential oils for scent (optional)
- Crayon pieces or wax dye for color (optional)

MATERIALS

- Twelve 125-gram (4-ounce) jam jars with canning lids and rings
- Twelve 4" large to extra-large waxed and wired wicks with tabs (such as HTP-126)

EQUIPMENT

- Double boiler
- Hot glue gun and glue or wax adhesive
- Thermometer
- Sharp scissors
- Kitchen scale
- Chopsticks or clothespins
- Old towel
- Paper cup
- Metal tray
- Heatproof container with pour spout

Tip: Soy wax can be dyed any color you want and takes to fragrance perfectly. Try making a large batch and switching up the scents and colors in different combinations. Soy wax also blends well with beeswax, which yields a smooth-textured, light golden, slightly sweet-smelling candle that captures the benefits of both soy wax and beeswax.

Fun for Everyone!

This project is suitable for even a beginning crafter. That means it's a great choice if you want to get a group together for a day of candle making, no experience necessary. Imagine a fun afternoon with the bridesmaids making a few dozen candles for an outdoor wedding. Pick your scent to personalize the candles, then dress them up with fabric and cord.

1 Assemble the double boiler and measure wax into the top pot. Heat over a medium heat setting, stirring regularly.

2 While the wax is melting, measure scent oil and prepare the crayons or wax dye (if using).

3 Prepare the jars by adding a bit of hot glue or wax adhesive to the bottom of the wick tabs and pressing them firmly into the centers of the jars. Place the jars on a metal tray or pan.

4 If you are adding color and scent, bring the wax to the specified temperature for adding dye or scent oil (for example, 160°F—see the instructions that came with your wax). Add color and scent and mix thoroughly to combine.

5 Cool the wax to 140°F and carefully pour it into the jars.

6 Prop up the wicks with chopsticks or clothespins to keep them centered. Wrap a towel around the outside of the tray or pan and set aside to cool. Be careful not to disturb the candles too much while they set. Once the candles are set, trim the wicks to ¼" above the wax.

To make these jam jars picture perfect, cut out a circle of fabric that is the diameter of the jar lid. Lay the fabric on the lid and secure the lid to the jar with the ring. Tie a bit of coordinating jute cord around the ring.

Lavender Candle

Makes one 450-gram (16-ounce) candle

Lavender (*Lavandula angustifolia*) is *the* herb of relaxation. These pressed herb candles add a beautiful, natural look and a heavenly scent that brings peace and serenity to any space. This design uses real herbs pressed on the inside of a glass canning jar as decoration. The wicks are a slightly thinner diameter than would normally be used for a wide-mouth jar like this; that way, the wax will not burn all the way to the sides of the jar, dislodging the pressed herbs. When the candle has burned all the way to the bottom of the jar, you can add a votive or tea light in its place and continue to enjoy the pressed lavender flowers and leaves on the jar.

INGREDIENTS

- 270 grams (9.5 ounces) soy wax for container candles
- 180 grams (6.3 ounces) beeswax pastilles
- 30 milliliters (1 ounce) lavender essential oil for scent (optional)
- Pressed young English lavender leaves and flower stems, with leaves and flowers no larger than 1" long and ½" wide (see step 1)

MATERIALS

- One 475-milliliter (16-fluid-ounce) wide-mouth glass canning jar
- One 6" large waxed and wired wick with tab (such as HTP-104)

EQUIPMENT

- Double boiler
- Hot glue gun and glue or wax adhesive
- Thermometer
- Sharp scissors
- Kitchen scale
- Paper cup
- Old towel
- Craft paintbrush
- Chopsticks or clothespins
- Heatproof container with pour spout

Lovely Lavender

Lavender is the herb of relaxation and serenity. It's a heavenly floral scent that helps you to wind down and de-stress. Try lighting one as part of your before-bed routine to soothe and relax you. Just make sure you blow out the candle before falling into a peaceful slumber.

1 Harvest young lavender flowers and leaves on thin green stems (not the older, woody stems with large flowers) and press them between heavy books or with a wooden press for a week, until they are very flat and dry. Cut the lavender stems so they will sit at least 1" below the rim of the jar.

2 Weigh the wax and melt in a double boiler with a thermometer attached. Measure the lavender oil in the paper cup and set aside.

3 Dip a pressed lavender bloom in the melted wax. Working quickly, place the stem on the inside of the jar; use the paintbrush to press it firmly in place as the wax cools. Brush melted wax over the lavender stem to hold it in place. Continue to add lavender stems around the inside of the jar, being sure that each is pressed completely flat on the jar.

4 When the lavender appliqués have dried, add a dab of hot glue or wax adhesive to attach the wick to the center bottom of the jar. Prop up the wick with a chopstick or clothespin to keep it centered.

5 If you are adding color and fragrance, bring the wax to the specified temperature for adding dye or scent oil (for example, 160°F—see the instructions that came with your wax). Add color and scent and mix thoroughly to combine. Cool the wax to 140°F and carefully pour into jars.

6 Wrap a towel around the outside of the jar and set aside to cool. Be careful not to disturb the candle too much while it sets. Once it has set, trim the wick to ¼" above the wax.

Add a lid to the jar and attach a chalkboard label to the top of the lid. Use a chalk marker so the message won't rub off easily (but it will come off with water and a cloth). Practice your script a few times before you add it to the label.

Summer Flowers Floating Candles

Makes six 30-gram (1-ounce) floating candles

Floating candles are a lovely way to add a little fire to a floral centerpiece and are surprisingly easy to make using metal tart molds. Made with sweet-smelling beeswax, these floral-shaped floating candles will be the buzz of the party.

INGREDIENTS

- 170 grams (6 ounces) beeswax

MATERIALS

- Six waxed and wired 1" tea light wicks with tabs
- Large, wide glass vase
- Fresh flowers

EQUIPMENT

- Double boiler
- Kitchen scale
- Baking sheet
- Heatproof container with pour spout
- Six mini metal tart molds

Tip: *When making candles in a container that you eventually want to remove, choose a wax formulated for votives or pillar candles or use a candle release additive to allow the wax to pop out of the mold more easily. If the wax doesn't release, pop the mold in the freezer for ten minutes, then try again. Keep freezing at ten-minute intervals until the candle can be removed. Just be sure not to leave the candle in the freezer for an extended period of time or it may crack.*

1 Measure and melt the beeswax in a double boiler. Keep a close watch on it so that it can be poured as soon as it's completely liquid.

2 Wipe out the tart molds to be sure the insides are quite clean. Place the tart molds on a baking sheet and place paper under the baking sheet to protect your countertop from spills.

How to Display Floating Candles

Floating candles sit right on the surface of water of a vase, glass, bathtub, or even a pond. To create a lavish display, fill a wide vase with freshly cut flowers and fill it with water to cover the blooms completely. The flowers will look great for a few days submerged in water. If the flowers try to float to the surface, pack a bunch of blooms and leaves into the vase, then add in a smaller floating glass vase filled with a bit of water to hold the candle.

3 Carefully pour wax into the tart molds, making sure that they stay level and that wax doesn't pour over the edges. When pouring a small volume of beeswax at a low temperature, the wax may cool and harden on the side of the pouring container. Put the container in the warm water of the double boiler to reliquefy as needed.

4 As the wax starts to cool and turn opaque around the edges, place a wick into the center of each candle. The wicks are short and should easily stay in place.

5 Let the candles cool and cure for twenty-four hours undisturbed, then remove them from the molds. Since the tart molds have sharp edges, hold each one with a dish cloth and gently pull the sides away from the candle. After a few snapping sounds, the candle will pop right out.

For a gift, why not pair these floating beeswax candles with a bouquet
of homegrown flowers? Arrange a few candles in a paper berry box and
give with a bouquet of freshly cut flowers tied with ribbon.

Seashell Tea Lights

Makes six 18-gram (0.6-ounce) tea lights

These delightful beeswax tea lights come from the ocean, but there are many other natural containers that can be used to make a candle. Walnut shells and acorn caps can be used using the methods shown in this project to make adorable tea lights.

INGREDIENTS

- 115 grams (4 ounces) beeswax

MATERIALS

- Eight medium-sized clam or oyster shells, deep enough to hold the same amount of wax as a standard tea light
- Eight waxed and wired 1" tea light wicks with tabs

EQUIPMENT

- Plastic tray/container large enough to hold all the shells
- Sand
- Double boiler
- Kitchen scale
- Heatproof container with pour spout

Visit an Underwater Garden

The ocean is a expansive ecosystem with many plants and animals that inhabit the depths. Using found seashells for a craft project has the benefit of time spent on a beach, enjoying the scents, sights, and sounds. Such a meditative act allows for peaceful reflection or rejuvenation.

1 Prepare the seashells by washing and drying them thoroughly.

2 Place the shells in a plastic tray filled with sand to hold them in place for pouring the wax. The sand will keep the shells in place while the wax sets.

3 Melt the beeswax in a double boiler. Keep a close watch on it so that it can be poured as soon as it is completely liquid.

4 Carefully pour wax into the shells, making sure that they stay level and that wax doesn't spill over the edges. As the wax starts to cool and turn opaque around the edges, place a wick in the center of each candle. The short wicks should easily stay in place.

5 Let the seashell tea lights cool and cure for twenty-four hours undisturbed.

A small bucket, reminiscent of a sand pail, will contain all of the seashell tea lights. A simple ribbon and tag make gift giving beautiful (and easy!).

Ombré Evergreen Candle

Makes one 225-gram (8-ounce) square candle

This modern ombré candle subtly nods to the holidays, making it a lovely winter accessory that doesn't date itself as soon as the festivities are over. The ombré effect is created with just one color of wax dye in different strengths to give the candle a decorative, graduated color that adds elegance and interest along with a pop of color while maintaining a minimalist style.

INGREDIENTS

- 225 grams (8 ounces) soy wax for container candles
- 15 milliliters (0.5 ounce) evergreen essential oil blend, divided into thirds (blend can include cypress, cedarwood, and sweet birch)
- One green dye chip for candle making (or the appropriate number of chips for the wax quantity)

MATERIALS

- One 3" x 3" x 3½" square glass candle jar
- One wood wick with metal tab

Tip: *The active time for this project isn't that much more than other candle projects. However, it does take a full day to complete this project because of the time for the wax to harden in between each layer. You can scale this project up or down to have as many layers as you would like, but keep in mind that the candle wax needs to harden completely before you pour the next layer.*

EQUIPMENT

- Double boiler
- Thermometer
- Kitchen scale
- Fine-tip pruning shears
- Hot glue gun and glue or wax adhesive
- Rubber gloves
- Old towel
- Heatproof container with pour spout
- Three paper cups or shot glasses

Color a Candle for Every Season

This candle has a spruce-inspired blue-green color that adds a modern touch to winter celebrations, but an ombré candle project can be done at any time of the year. Change it up depending on the season. For the spring, use pretty pastels. For summer, use bold jewel tones. And for fall, use warm colors like yellow, orange, and red. You can also swap out the fragrance to match the seasonal colors.

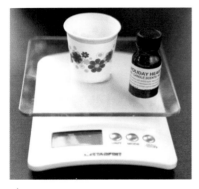

1 Weigh the soy wax and add it to a double boiler on medium heat. While the wax is melting, measure the fragrance or essential oil into three paper cups equally. Then prepare the dye chips.

2 Prepare the wood wick by determining its final height in the candle, ¼" above the top of the wax. Feed the wooden wick into the metal base and use a dab of hot glue or wax adhesive to attach it to the bottom of the jar at the center.

3 Prepare your ombré colors by calculating how much dye will be needed for the amount of wax. Then, divide the dye chip into three pieces: one large, one medium, and one small. A larger difference between the sizes of the chips will mean a greater difference in the color of each wax layer. Use rubber gloves to protect your hands from the dye while you're cutting the chip.

4 Add each piece of dye chip to a shot glass and top with hot wax. Use a chopstick to stir and dissolve the dye chip completely. If the dye chip doesn't completely dissolve, you can place the shot glass in the double boiler to heat it up a bit more.

5 When the melted wax has reached the specified temperature for adding dye or scent oil (for example, 160°F—see the instructions that came with your wax), pour a third of the wax into a heatproof measuring cup, add the wax you dissolved the largest dye chip in, and pour in one-third of the scent oil. Stir well to combine.

6 Cool the wax to 140°F and pour it into the jar. Leave it untouched to set for at least one hour. It could take longer than an hour for the wax layer to set, depending on the temperature in the room that you're working in.

Wrap the candle with a piece of jute twine and insert a freshly cut sprig of evergreen between the bow and the candle glass. The simple and natural wrapping allows for the gorgeous ombré to peek through, ready to be revealed completely when the twine has been removed (shown on page 124).

7 Follow steps 5–6 for the remaining two layers, adding the scent oil and the wax with the dissolved medium chip first and then the wax with the dissolved small chip. Pour each layer only when the previous layer is completely set.

Tip: You can trim the candle wick using the fine-tip pruning shears after the candle is poured, but you'll get a cleaner cut if you measure and trim the wick before you pour the candle. Also, when using a wood wick and a square jar, align the wick so that it is centered within the square.

Aromatherapy

Aromatherapy is the holistic practice of using the scent of plants as part of health and wellness. You may have heard that scent is deeply connected to memory and emotion. This is because the part of the brain that processes smells, the limbic system, is the same part that processes memory and emotion. This type of herbal therapy has been around for longer than me, or you, or Western medicine for that matter.

You can access therapeutic plant aromas by infusing or steeping dried or fresh plants to release the volatile oils. The aroma that is released from a cup of herbal tea or an herb-infused vinegar comes from those oils. It's not difficult to enjoy the scent of plants! It can be as simple as bruising plant leaves and rubbing them in your hands to release the fragrance.

Essential oils are a condensed, bottled form of these plant oils. While infusions and steeping herbs are used to scent many of the projects of this book, essential oils are also a great way to add scent. The previous chapter goes into more detail on how to use essential oils to scent candles.

There are a few things to note when seeking out essential oils for personal use.

- The fact that these oils are derived from plants does not mean all bodies will react the same to them. Avoid placing place pure essential oils directly on skin without diluting them in a carrier oil, and never ingest essential oils.

- There is no certification or industry standard for essential oils, meaning the quality is all over the map. I look for highly rated herb companies who value sustainability, fair trade, organic agriculture, and high quality. Look for proper botanical names and educational information and be educated about precautions.

- More expensive oils are not necessarily better—some expensive brands have far inferior products than some lower-priced brands. Yes, ingredients are one reason for the price of a bottle, but that number is also influenced by marketing, customer demand, and supply scale, among other things.

- Beware of any company that claims essential oils can cure disease or makes medical promises. If you have a specific health issue, seek the advice of a medical professional and avoid marketing statements.

Essential Oil Scent Blends

One of the most fun things to do with aromatherapy is to mix the oils to create your own blends! Here are some of my favorites.

GOOD MORNING

1 part cinnamon bark essential oil

1 part sweet orange essential oil

1 part vanilla absolute*

*Note: Absolutes or oleoresins are often used in the same way as essential oils, but they are extracted using a solvent rather than distillation. Vanilla extract is not a substitute for absolute or essential oils.

SLEEPY TIME

2 parts lavender essential oil

1 part sweet orange essential oil

SUMMER FLOWERS

1 part lavender essential oil

1 part geranium essential oil

1 part rose essential oil

EVERGREEN

1 part cypress essential oil

1 part cedarwood essential oil

1 part sweet birch essential oil

VITALITY

3 parts lavender essential oil

2 parts mandarin essential oil

1 part lemongrass essential oil

1 part geranium essential oil

1 part ylang-ylang essential oil

1 part patchouli essential oil

PUMPKIN SPICE

2 parts cinnamon bark essential oil

2 parts sweet orange essential oil

1 part cardamom essential oil

1 part nutmeg essential oil

1 part ginger essential oil

1 part clove essential oil

CITRUS CELEBRATION

1 part lime essential oil

1 part lemon essential oil

1 part grapefruit essential oil

1 part sweet orange essential oil

1 part tangerine essential oil

Soaps & Sanitizers
What does "clean" really mean?

A sparkling shine? A fresh scent? A squeaky feeling? Or is it about safety—removing contaminants that can cause illness? No matter what clean means to you, I'm sure you'd prefer the process to be free from harsh chemicals, excess effort, and high costs. That's where these botanical green cleaning recipes come in!

Making cleaners, sanitizers, and soaps at home takes us back to a simpler time with less packaging, less effort, and fewer products—to a time when a bit of alcohol, vinegar, water, plant-based soap, and herbs were all you needed to clean and sanitize your home and body. The beauty of herbal cleaning products is that you know you aren't washing away grime with a long list of unrecognizable ingredients. Instead, you can choose your ingredients, customize the scents, and save money.

The diverse recipes included here feature common, natural ingredients as well as therapeutic scents, skin-soothing properties, and natural cleansers direct from Mother Earth. I hope these recipes launch you into a world of botanical cleaning that will keep your family safe, your skin healthy, and your home smelling like a garden!

Getting Started

In this section, I will dig deeper into the ingredients so you have a solid foundation before you start mixing. Many natural ingredients have cleansing, disinfecting, antibacterial, or antifungal properties that make them ideal for DIY cleaning products. You may be familiar with some of these ingredients, while others may surprise you. Let's take a closer look at the items you can use for cleaning and what makes them great cleansers and sanitizers. I'll also touch on the shelf life of your finished products and safety tips. Armed with the recipes and knowledge of the ingredients, you can begin to customize the cleaners by using your preferred herbs and essential oils. Ready to get clean?

Ingredients

BLEACH ALTERNATIVES

Bleach may be a popular ingredient in commercial sanitizers and cleaners, but it's highly toxic. It's an irritant to both the lungs and skin, making cleaning with it a hazard. The good news? Many other household cleaners that you can use instead of bleach are safe, effective, and easy to find.

VINEGAR: Vinegar is acetic acid, which is effective at cleaning soap scum, grime, and stains. As long as it is diluted, vinegar can be used on multiple surfaces to disinfect and clean them safely. However, the same action that removes dirt and stains can dull the finish of shiny or porous materials like granite, some tiles, and hardwood. Vinegar cleaner remains a good option for tubs, toilets, kitchen appliances, and windows. There are many types of vinegar available in the grocery store, from balsamic vinegar to apple cider vinegar. For cleaning, use inexpensive white vinegar—save the other ones for your salads.

BAKING SODA: Baking soda or sodium bicarbonate is on the opposite side of the pH scale from vinegar. Its alkaline properties allow it to remove dirt and grease. It is also an excellent deodorizer. Baking soda absorbs aromas, so you can use it in the fridge, garbage can, or litter box to eliminate unpleasant scents. To remove odors from carpets and upholstery, sprinkle on baking soda liberally and leave it overnight. In the morning, vacuum it up. Because baking soda is abrasive, you can mix it with water to form a paste that you can use to scrub away at tough dirt. Be careful not to scratch surfaces, though, and always do a small spot test before scrubbing a larger area.

ISOPROPYL ALCOHOL: Isopropyl alcohol is sold as a mixture of isopropanol and water. It is labeled based on the amount of alcohol it contains, like 70% or 99.9%. This type of alcohol is readily absorbed into the skin and can be toxic at high doses. The purest form (99.9%) of isopropyl alcohol evaporates quickly and can be breathed into your lungs. When it is denatured

A Note about Alcohol

Most natural cleaners and sanitizers can be made with ingredients that are safe for the skin and nontoxic. However, to kill viruses, health authorities recommend a solution of at least 60% to 70% alcohol. So, if you want to make a sanitizer that will reduce your chances of catching viruses, it's necessary to include alcohol. All of the recipes in this book that use isopropyl alcohol contain other ingredients to counteract some of the alcohol's less desirable effects. When using isopropyl alcohol in these recipes, it's important to do a spot check on your skin or the surface you're cleaning first and wait twenty-four hours for a reaction. Use these products in moderation, and be sure to get approval and advice from your health care professional. Be smart, be safe, and use them with care.

with additives like water, the alcohol content is reduced to between 68% and 72%, and it is sold as rubbing alcohol. Rubbing alcohol is used as a medical antiseptic and industrial disinfectant and is generally considered safe for home use in small amounts. See the sidebar on the facing page for more information about why you may want to incorporate isopropyl alcohol into your green cleaners.

VODKA: Ethanol, found in grain alcohol or vodka, is a gentler alcohol disinfectant than isopropyl alcohol. Ethanol is a natural byproduct of plant fermentation, and the alcohol content varies. Vodka, for instance, is typically around 40% alcohol. At that concentration, it will not kill viruses, but it is still an exceptional disinfectant.

HYDROGEN PEROXIDE: Hydrogen peroxide is also a chemical compound that is usually diluted and sold as a mild antiseptic at around 3% concentration. Small amounts of it can be used as a surface cleaner or topically on wounds. However, it is not to be used on deep or severe wounds or burns.

LEMONS, CITRUS, AND CITRIC ACID: Lemons and other citrus fruits contain citric acid, which acts as vinegar does to clean. It is a mild antiseptic and antibacterial and also removes stains. Like vinegar, it can be tough on porous surfaces and finishes, so it is not recommended for hardwood, granite, or natural stone.

LAVENDER: Lavender (*Lavandula angustifolia*) is a herbal antiseptic and oil solvent that excels at cleansing and soothing the skin. Lavender's gentle fragrance is used in aromatherapy to promote calm, but its cleaning power packs a punch! Adding lavender essential oil to recipes is beneficial for your skin and the surfaces you're cleaning. It's wonderful in the shower to prevent mildew and ideal in hand soap to speed skin repair. Add dried lavender buds to a muslin bag and toss it in your pillowcase, sock drawer, or dryer to add a fresh scent to linens. As a bonus, it can also be used as an insect repellant.

TEA TREE: Tea tree (*Melaleuca alternifolia*) oil is used as an antifungal and antiseptic skin treatment, but it is also used for cleaning and deodorizing around the house. A few drops of tea tree oil can be used when cleaning the toilet bowl, washing machine, coffee maker, and garbage disposal. It also works wonders on musty towels, dish rags, and pet bedding.

CASTILE SOAP: Castile soap is a specific olive oil soap that comes from Castile, Spain. For the recipes in this book, Castile soap refers to any plant-based liquid soap. It can be made from olive, coconut, avocado, or other plant oils. This biodegradable, nontoxic soap comes as a concentrate, so it should be diluted to the proper level according to the recipe. I always choose an unscented soap as my base and add my own essential oils.

OTHER INGREDIENTS

ALOE: Aloe vera (*Aloe barbadensis*) is one of the oldest plants on record to be noted for healing properties. It has been cultivated worldwide due to its highly adaptable nature and usefulness as a skin-healing herb. Aloe is a natural antibacterial and contains antiseptics that help clean cuts and wounds. Aloe's pH level closely matches that of our skin, enabling it to gently (but thoroughly) cleanse skin while also closing the pores. Its anti-inflammatory qualities can calm inflamed skin. All of this makes aloe a fabulous ingredient in soaps and sanitizers.

WITCH HAZEL: Witch hazel (*Hamamelis* spp.) earned its name because it was once popularly used for water witching, using a branch to locate water underground. Today, witch hazel is prized for its anti-inflammatory and skincare properties. A cotton bandage soaked in witch hazel can be frozen to create a cold compress for wounds and stitches. A spritz of witch hazel on your skin after a shower helps tone skin and reduce redness and inflammation.

VEGETABLE GLYCERIN: After you use a bar of natural soap, you may feel like you didn't wash all of it off your skin. That silky coating left behind is glycerin. In commercial soap (which is technically not soap but a detergent), the glycerin is often removed and repackaged because it is more valuable on its own. Then, artificial moisturizers are added to the soap to replicate the glycerin's silky texture. Vegetable glycerin is made from plants like coconut, palm, and soy. When added to non-soap sanitizers, it can help protect and repair skin.

ESSENTIAL OILS: Essential oils are the concentrated herbal oils from a variety of plants. Claims that essential oils kill viruses and cure diseases are irresponsible and can be dangerous, but, sadly, they are common. Think of these oils as a fine liqueur—just a few drops can add fragrance and herbal properties to home cleaning products. It's important to use essential oils with caution and in the way they are intended: in small amounts, heavily diluted, and never ingested. In this way, essential oils can add a lot of benefits to natural home cleaners, soaps, and sanitizers. But most of all, they'll make your recipes smell terrific and can offer you some aromatherapy as you use them.

HERBS: Fresh and dried herbs contain many cleansing and sanitizing properties. Because they are much less concentrated than essential oils, they are also much safer to use in recipes. Infusing vinegar with citrus rinds and fresh herbs is a wonderful way to add fragrance and herbal properties to a recipe, boosting its effectiveness and your enjoyment in using the finished product.

Shelf Life

As with the other projects in this book, the expiry date of a product you make at home will be the earliest expiry date of the ingredients you use to make the recipe. For instance, if your recipe calls for an ingredient that expires in six months and another that expires in one year, the final product will expire in six months.

That said, any ingredients that contain water are more susceptible to spoilage and microbial growth. Aloe vera, witch hazel, fresh herbs, citrus rinds, and any other organic ingredients will decrease the shelf life of your cleaning products.

Avoid contamination by sterilizing bottles, equipment, and surfaces before mixing your products, and always wash your hands thoroughly before and after mixing.

Keep in mind that other factors may impact shelf life, such as temperature, storage conditions, sanitation when preparing the recipes, and the quality of the ingredients. Your best bet is to make recipes in small batches and discard any products that have taken on a different appearance, color, or smell since you created them. Store finished products in a cool, dark space when not in use.

Safety

As with any product you use on your skin, it's important to know if you have any allergies or intolerances to the ingredients. The same is true for the surfaces in your home. Before the widespread use of any product, test it on a small area of your skin or home surface.

For skin, test the product on the inside of your elbow and wait twenty-four hours to see if there is a reaction. For home surfaces, test the cleaner on a small, hidden spot. Wait twenty-four hours, then check to see if the cleaner caused any dulling or discoloration.

Above all else, use common sense and follow your health care professional's guidance for your individual health needs.

Tools

For the recipes in this section, you will need a basic assortment of general kitchen implements such as measuring cups, funnels, mason jars, bowls, strainers, scissors, and spoons. These recipes require slightly less precision than the skin and body apothecary or candle recipes, so there is a little more flexibility if you want to adapt ingredient measurements to the tools you have, but you should still try to be precise and make sure to account for different materials' weights/masses if converting from weight or mass to volume or vice versa.

Basil & Bergamot-Scented Moisturizing Liquid Hand Soap

Makes 500 milliliters (approximately 2 cups) of soap

Whenever you find yourself washing your hands repeatedly, like during cold and flu season, it is increasingly important to add moisture back into the skin. Dry skin isn't just uncomfortable; it also breaks down the skin's protective barrier. As our skin breaks down, it is more prone to cuts, rashes, sores, and pulled cuticles, all of which provide entry points for germs. This liquid hand soap is made with gentle Castile soap along with moisturizing oil to help soften skin.

INGREDIENTS

- 400 milliliters distilled or boiled water
- 100 milliliters unscented concentrated liquid Castile soap
- 1 tablespoon liquid oil (olive oil, almond oil, or avocado oil)
- 10 drops basil essential oil
- 10 drops bergamot essential oil

MATERIALS

- 500-milliliter bottle with soap pump

EQUIPMENT

- Measuring cups
- Funnel

Basil & Bergamot

Basil (Ocimum basilicum) is often used on the skin to help repair, balance, and nourish it. Bergamot (Citrus bergamia) is often used for its antibacterial and anti-inflammatory properties, which help to calm skin. It also adds a pleasant floral citrus scent to this liquid soap recipe.

1 Measure and combine the water and Castile soap.

2 Add the liquid oil and essential oils.

3 Use the funnel to pour the mixture into the bottle.

4 Cap the bottle and shake well to combine.

How to Use

Shake well before each use for the first few days. Over time, the ingredients will combine permanently, and shaking will no longer be necessary. Apply one or two pumps of soap to wet hands and lather for twenty seconds. Use a nail brush to remove any dirt hiding under your nails. Rinse well and dry with a clean towel.

Lime & Rosemary–Scented Foaming Hand Soap

Makes 400 milliliters (approximately 1¾ cups) of soap

Foaming hand soap feels luxurious on your skin. It comes out of the pump already lathered up, so it's silky and smooth. If you like a good, bubbly lather, this foaming soap recipe is for you. As an added bonus, it has a fabulous bright lime and rosemary scent.

Foaming soap is 60% water, 20% prepared liquid soap, and 20% air. You can scale this recipe up or down based on this ratio to make as much or as little soap as you need.

While I love foaming hand soap, especially for use with children, keep in mind that working soap into a lather helps draw dirt from your skin into the bubbles, which are then washed away. Simply rubbing foam soap on your hands and then rinsing them immediately is not going to clean them as well as if you work the soap into a lather. Completely work the soap into your hands as if you're using liquid soap.

INGREDIENTS

- 375 milliliters distilled or boiled water
- 25 milliliters unscented concentrated liquid Castile soap
- 20 drops lime essential oil
- 10 drops rosemary essential oil

MATERIALS

- 500-milliliter mason jar with foaming soap pump attachment

EQUIPMENT

- Measuring cups

Rosemary & Lime

Rosemary (Rosmarinus officinalis) is said to control oil production and has an antibacterial quality. As a natural antioxidant, lime (Citrus aurantiifolia) can help remove free radicals that damage cells, causing wrinkles, sunspots, and other signs of aging.

1 Fill the mason jar with the water.

2 Add the Castile soap.

3 Add the essential oils.

4 Cap the jar and shake well to combine.

How to Use

Shake well before each use for the first few days. Over time, the ingredients will combine permanently, and shaking will no longer be necessary. Apply one or two pumps of soap to wet hands and scrub for twenty seconds, working the soap over the front and back of your hands and between your fingers. When used this way, foaming soap is just as effective as liquid or bar soap.

Aloe & Witch Hazel Hand Sanitizer Gel

Makes 240 milliliters (approximately 1 cup) of sanitizer

In the past, I generally avoided hand sanitizers, preferring to wash my hands with soap and water to remove germs and viruses. However, sanitizer is great to have on hand when you're out and about.

Over the years, I've become somewhat of a hand sanitizer connoisseur, and you may be too! You'll find that some feel slimy and others sticky, some have an overpowering fragrance, and others are terribly drying.

This hand sanitizer is designed to feel great on your skin, smell wonderful, and do an effective job of cleaning when soap and water are not available. **It is formulated to clean without water, not to combat viruses.** It simulates handwashing when there is no water and soap available (see the alcohol-based hand sanitizer recipe on page 152 for more information).

The ingredients are good for your skin, and the plants have beneficial properties for cleansing. By adding hand sanitizer to your personal cleaning routine, your hands and skin will thank you.

INGREDIENTS

- 80 milliliters pure witch hazel
- 160 milliliters 100% pure aloe vera gel
- 10 drops lavender essential oil
- 2.5 milliliters (½ teaspoon) vitamin E oil

MATERIALS

- Two 125-milliliter bottles with soap pumps

EQUIPMENT

- Measuring cups
- Small bowl
- Funnel

1 Mix the witch hazel and aloe vera gel together in a bowl.

2 Add the essential oil and mix well. Then add the vitamin E oil and stir well to combine.

3 Use the funnel to pour the mixture into the bottles.

4 Cap the bottles and shake well to combine.

How to Use

Massage a dollop of hand sanitizer into your skin, rubbing it all over your hands and between your fingers as if you were washing them with soap. Afterward, if possible, use water to rinse your hands, and dry them thoroughly.

SHELF LIFE: Aloe gel hand sanitizer will last up to the expiry date of the aloe vera. This could be up to a year if stored properly in a cool location like the fridge. In the absence of expiry dates, or when using fresh aloe vera, discard aloe gel sanitizer after seven to ten days, or sooner if it shows signs of spoilage.

Alcohol-Based Hand Sanitizer Spray

Makes 200 milliliters (approximately ¾ cup) of sanitizer

It only takes a few ingredients and just minutes to put together this alcohol-based hand sanitizer. This spray sanitizer can be used on both hands and surfaces in a pinch.

Public health officials recommend that hand sanitizer contain at least 60% alcohol to eliminate viruses, bacteria, and other germs. This recipe is more than 70% alcohol. It's not as moisturizing as the aloe hand sanitizer on page 148, but it is an alcohol-based option for when you need it.

Even though this alcohol-based recipe is harsher on the skin than the aloe version, I still prefer this homemade alcohol-based sanitizer over commercial options because the addition of glycerin and witch hazel does help soften skin. Plus, adding essential oils helps mitigate the strong smell of isopropyl alcohol. The alcohol aroma will dissipate quickly, but the scent of sweet orange and lavender will linger on your hands.

INGREDIENTS

- 140 milliliters 99.9% isopropyl alcohol
- 25 milliliters vegetable glycerin
- 25 milliliters witch hazel
- 4 drops sweet orange essential oil
- 4 drops lavender essential oil
- 4 drops tea tree oil

MATERIALS

- Two 100-milliliter spray bottles

EQUIPMENT

- Measuring cups
- Funnel

Choose Soap & Water First

The best way to keep your hands clean is to wash them with soap and water regularly. Whenever washing is not possible, this hand sanitizer provides an alternative, portable option.

1 Add the glycerin and witch hazel to the alcohol.

2 Add the essential oils.

3 Use the funnel to pour the mixture into the bottles.

4 Cap the bottles and shake well to combine.

How to Use

Shake well before each use. Add a spray or two of sanitizer to your hands. Rub it all over your hands and between your fingers as if you were washing them with soap. Afterward, if possible, use water to rinse your hands. Apply moisturizer regularly.

Isopropyl alcohol is readily absorbed into the skin, so it's best to use it sparingly. In small amounts, there is not usually a negative reaction, but some skin may be more sensitive. Always do a small test first and watch for adverse reactions such as a rash, redness, drying, or cracking skin.

SHELF LIFE: The alcohol content in this recipe will prevent bacterial and mold growth. However, its potency will wane over time. Discard any unused sanitizer after one year to be safe.

Travel Disinfecting Wipes

Makes 30 wipes

Even though these disinfecting wipes are made with pretty cocktail napkins, don't let them fool you—they're still powerful enough to effectively clean your hands or surfaces. Keep them in a metal storage container and toss them in your bag so they're handy whenever you need them.

When you open the travel container, you will certainly be hit by the alcohol aroma. But once you rub a wipe on your hands, that will quickly dissipate, leaving behind the softness of the coconut oil and the scent of lavender and lemon.

INGREDIENTS

- 350 milliliters 70% isopropyl alcohol (or dilute 99.9% isopropyl alcohol to 70% using distilled water)
- 15 milliliters (1 tablespoon) fractionated coconut oil
- 3 drops lavender essential oil
- 3 drops lemon essential oil

MATERIALS

- Thirty 5" x 5" folded cocktail napkins
- 6" x 4" stainless steel food storage container with snap-on lid

EQUIPMENT

- Measuring cups

Lavender & Lemon Magic

The combination of these two popular essential oil fragrances is one of my favorites. Calming, floral lavender and uplifting, bright lemon work together to leave a pleasant scent on your hands once the alcohol dissipates.

1 Fold all the napkins in half so they fit in the container.

2 Mix the alcohol and coconut oil. Then add the essential oils.

3 Place the folded napkins in the container and pour the mixture over them.

4 With clean hands, press down on the napkins to ensure they're evenly saturated with the alcohol mixture. Close the container, add a label, and your wipes are ready to use.

How to Use

Remove a wipe from the container and thoroughly rub it over your hands or the surface you want to clean. Discard the used wipe. Do not flush it or add it to green waste.

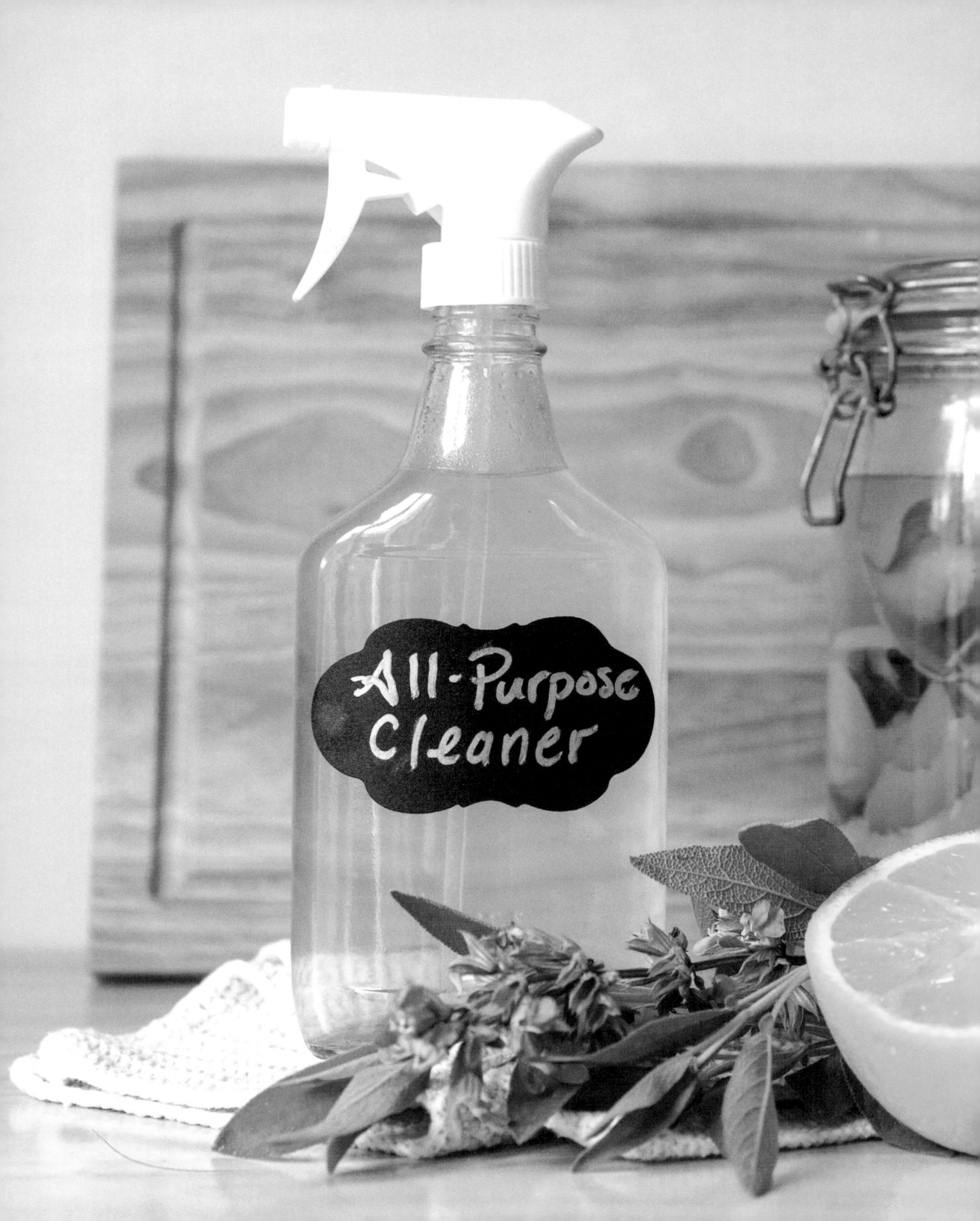
All-Purpose
Cleaner

Orange & Sage All-Purpose Cleaner

Makes 1.5 liters (approximately 1½ quarts) of concentrated vinegar cleaner

The ingredients in this recipe could be used to dress a fresh salad, but they also have powerful cleaning properties!

Vinegar has been used throughout the ages for home cleaning because of its acidity. The acetic acid counteracts oil, soap, dirt, and sticky messes around the house. It also helps disinfect surfaces. The only thing I don't love about vinegar as a cleaner is that it doesn't smell that great. Combining orange peels and fresh garden sage with vinegar adds even more cleaning power and a beautiful fragrance that makes your house smell clean. You could also choose to replace the orange and sage with lemon balm (*Melissa officinalis*).

This cleaner is strong enough yet gentle enough to be used throughout the house, from kitchen counters to sticky stovetops, to the bathroom, and even to mop the floors. The finished product is a concentrate that you can dilute based on the strength you need. Keep the concentration high for difficult cleaning projects and dilute it for light cleaning.

INGREDIENTS

- 4–5 large oranges, peeled
- A handful of fresh sage leaves
- 1½ liters distilled white vinegar
- Sage essential oil (optional)

MATERIALS

- Spray bottle

EQUIPMENT

- Measuring cups
- Strainer
- 2-liter mason jar with lid

Orange & Sage

*Orange has a wonderfully uplifting scent that makes us feel cheery and bright. The orange oil found in the peels also has cleaning properties. Sage (*Salvia officinalis*) is packed with antifungal and antibacterial properties. The ancient Greeks and Romans preserved meat with sage because of its ability to reduce bacteria. It makes a great addition to this all-purpose cleaner.*

1 Add the orange peels and sage to the mason jar.

2 Top off the jar with the vinegar and keep it covered in a cool, dark place for one week.

3 After a week, strain the liquid into another jar, bowl, or measuring cup.

4 If you'd like a stronger herb smell, add a few drops of sage essential oil. Store the concentrate in a clean jar until you are ready to dilute it for use.

How to Use

This homemade cleaner is all-purpose and perfect for bathrooms, kitchens, and floors.

Make a strong grease and soap scum cleaner for stovetops and bathrooms by combining one part vinegar concentrate with one part water in the spray bottle.

Make an all-purpose kitchen counter spray by combining one part vinegar concentrate with three parts water in the spray bottle.

Add ½ cup of vinegar concentrate to 1 gallon of warm water for mopping laminate and tile floors. For hardwood floors, don't use the vinegar concentrate. Instead, add 1 tablespoon of undiluted Castile soap to 1 gallon of warm water.

SHELF LIFE: Use within six weeks. I recommend making small batches so you always have some fresh cleaner on hand.

Lemongrass & Pine Alcohol-Based Disinfecting Kitchen Cleaner

Makes 880 milliliters (approximately 1 quart) of cleaner

Vinegar is a wonderful all-purpose cleaner, but it's not for granite or stone countertops. It's too acidic and will wear away the lovely finish of those surfaces, making them dull and lifeless. This alcohol-based cleaner is much gentler on your home surfaces, suitable for granite and stone, but is still tough on surface messes.

For this recipe, you can use any inexpensive, clear alcohol. I chose vodka and avoided the top-shelf brands. Vodka is only around 40% alcohol, which makes this recipe around 8% alcohol. This isn't sufficient to kill viruses but is good for disinfecting counters. If you'd like to increase the alcohol content of this recipe, use 99.9% isopropyl alcohol, which will bring the final product to 20% alcohol. If you want to sanitize a counter by using at least 60% alcohol to address viruses, use the alcohol-based hand sanitizer (page 152) or travel wipes (page 156) instead.

INGREDIENTS

- 700 milliliters water
- 175 milliliters clear alcohol (vodka or 99.9% isopropyl alcohol)
- 8 drops unscented concentrated liquid Castile soap
- 5 drops lemongrass essential oil
- 5 drops pine essential oil

MATERIALS

- 1-liter spray bottle

EQUIPMENT

- Measuring cups

Fresh & Clean with Lemongrass & Pine

Lemongrass (Cymbopogon *spp.*) essential oil is long-lasting with a strong scent. In some recipes, it can outshine and mask the other scents, which is exactly what makes it so appropriate in this recipe. Just a few drops give this cleaner the power to neutralize kitchen and bathroom smells. Pine (Pinus *spp.*) is a disinfectant that leaves a fresh, clean scent behind and pairs well with the earthiness of lemongrass.

1 Measure the water and alcohol.

2 Add the water, alcohol, and Castile soap to the spray bottle.

3 Add the essential oils.

4 Cap the bottle and shake well to combine.

How to Use

Shake well before each use. Spray counters and wipe with a soft cloth.

NOTE: On stone counters, it's recommended to avoid using abrasive cleaners and tools like scrubby sponges, steel wool, and even baking soda. Granite can actually be scratched, so only use soft cloths and this alcohol cleaner recipe.

Reusable Lemon & Rosemary–Scented Kitchen & Bathroom Wipes

Makes 16 reusable wipes

Use these reusable wipes to cut grease, grab grime, and remove soap scum with one fresh-smelling swipe of your hand. They look pretty enough to keep on the countertop, where they're easy to grab for quick cleanups. The wipes are reusable, so toss them in the laundry when you're finished, and they'll be ready for the next round of cleaning!

INGREDIENTS

- 120 milliliters water
- 120 milliliters vinegar
- 10 milliliters (2 teaspoons) unscented concentrated liquid Castile soap
- 10 drops lemon essential oil
- 10 drops rosemary essential oil

MATERIALS

- Two 30" x 30" muslin fabric squares
- Large jar with lid

EQUIPMENT

- Measuring cups
- Scissors

Lemon & Rosemary Forever

Lemon is the scent of clean. Its bright aroma does the job but doesn't linger too long, leaving behind only freshness. Rosemary is an excellent herb for deodorizing while adding an earthy, calming scent. Combined with lemon, it balances this recipe well for both kitchen and bathroom cleaning.

1 Take one of the muslin squares and fold it in half. Then fold it in half again lengthwise so you end up with a 30" x 7½" rectangle.

2 Cut the fabric at the folds to create four 30" x 7½" strips.

3 Fold each strip in half widthwise and cut at the fold again to create eight 7½" x 15" wipes.

4 Repeat steps 1–3 with the remaining muslin square to make eight more wipes. Place all 16 wipes in the jar.

5 Measure the water in a measuring cup. Add the Castile soap and gently stir to dissolve. Then add the vinegar and essential oils. (Note: Be sure to add the soap before the vinegar. Otherwise, it will clump and be difficult to dissolve.)

6 Pour the mixture over the wipes. With clean hands, press down on the wipes to ensure they're evenly saturated with the mixture. Cover the jar with the lid.

How to Use

Remove one wipe from the jar and use it to clean counters, sinks, and appliances. When finished, toss the wipe in the wash. Laundered wipes can be used again with fresh cleaning solution.

The wipes can be washed and reused repeatedly, but the cleaning solution should be replaced every three months. When removing wipes from the jar, be sure your hands are clean to avoid contamination, and be careful to touch only one wipe.

Fruit & Vegetable Wash

Makes 600 milliliters (approximately 2½ cups) of fruit and vegetable wash

A wash made of acid and salt makes it easy to remove some of the waxes, chemical sprays, and dirt that can stick to produce when it comes home from the grocery store. The ingredients in this fruit and vegetable wash help get produce squeaky clean without adding an off-putting flavor.

Vegetables and fruit usually have some sort of microorganisms on them. In most cases, washing produce prolongs its life by removing these organisms. However, some fruit and vegetables have their own natural protective measures. For example, blueberries have bloom, a fine, powdery covering that fights off the bacteria and fungus that would cause premature decay.

Most fruit and vegetables can be washed when they come home from the grocery store, but in some cases, you should wait to wash them until just before eating in order to prolong their shelf life.

INGREDIENTS

- 475 milliliters warm water
- 120 milliliters white vinegar
- 2 tablespoons citric acid
- 2 tablespoons salt

MATERIALS

- Spray bottle

EQUIPMENT

- Measuring cups

1 Measure the warm water.

2 Add the citric acid and salt and stir until both are fully dissolved.

3 Pour the water mixture and vinegar into the spray bottle.

How to Use

Spray your produce to cover all surfaces, let the spray rest for two minutes, and then rinse it off with tap water before consuming the food.

While this fruit and vegetable wash does taste rather good (if you like salt and vinegar chips), it will not change or affect the flavor of the produce. As long as it's applied as directed, even soft-skinned fruit like strawberries and raspberries will not take on the salt and vinegar flavor.

Tea Tree & Peppermint Toilet Bombs

Makes 16–20 ice cube–sized toilet bombs

If cleaning the toilet is not your favorite job, let these toilet bombs do the work for you! Keep a container of these fresh-scented cleaners in the bathroom, and pop one in the toilet when the bowl needs a refresh. They will fizz and bubble, releasing the cleaning ingredients and a fresh scent. They can also be used in sink drains and garbage disposals. Just pop one of these in the drain, and it will fizz away any grease, buildup, and stinky odors that may be lingering.

INGREDIENTS

- 2 cups baking soda
- 1 cup citric acid
- 10 drops tea tree essential oil
- 10 drops peppermint essential oil
- 60 milliliters unscented concentrated liquid Castile soap
- 240 milliliters water

MATERIALS

- Jar with lid

EQUIPMENT

- Spray bottle
- Silicone ice cube mold (optional)
- Measuring cups
- Mixing bowl
- Spatula
- Parchment paper

Now That's Fresh!

Tea tree and peppermint are both superior at deodorizing. Tea tree has antifungal and antiseptic properties, and it's hard to beat the freshness that goes along with the scent of peppermint. This cheery combination will add some pep to the job of cleaning the toilet!

1 Add the baking soda and citric acid to a bowl and mix with a spatula. Add the essential oils and mix them in well.

2 Combine the Castile soap and water in the spray bottle. Spray this solution lightly on top of the powder mixture, mixing it in quickly with your hands as you spritz. Continue to spray the powder and mix until it packs together easily in your hands like a snowball. (Note: You will not need all the Castile soap and water mixture for this recipe. The amount varies and should be judged by how the mixture forms.)

3 Press the mixture into a silicone ice cube mold. If you don't have a mold, roll the mixture into balls about the size of ice cubes.

4 Allow the mixture to set until firm, then pop the pieces out of the mold. Set the toilet bombs on parchment paper and allow them to dry until they feel firm. Store them in the jar.

How to Use

Store the toilet bombs in a jar and pop one out when you need to refresh your bathtub, sink, or toilet. Simply toss one into the toilet bowl and watch as it fizzes away, leaving the toilet clean and smelling fresh.

Use toilet bombs in the evening before going to bed for a fresh, clean bowl every morning. Or use them as needed between cleanings with an all-purpose cleaner.

These toilet bombs will last for years and still fizz as soon as they hit the water, but the essential oil fragrance will dissipate after a few months. Store them in a sealed jar to keep the scent from evaporating.

Keeping Things Fresh

Switching to green cleaning shouldn't be a chore!

With just a few basics—liquid soap, vinegar cleaner, alcohol cleaner, and cleaning bombs—you can freshen up your home quickly. Here are a few of my favorite ways to bring botanicals into your usual cleaning routine.

- Start your good night in the morning! I always make my bed in the morning, but before I do, I spritz a bit of lavender linen water on the sheets. Make lavender water with 950 milliliters (4 cups) of distilled water, 60 milliliters (¼ cup) of witch hazel, and 25 drops of lavender essential oil. Shake well before each use.

- Replace dryer sheets with lavender dryer bags! To make, add dried lavender buds into drawstring muslin bags (typically sold as bouquet garni bags). Toss a bag in with the laundry to add a light fragrance; the bag will last for 10 loads. These can also be used as drawer and closet fresheners or tucked into a pillowcase to release scent while you sleep. Add dried mint and hops to the lavender buds for sweeter dreams.

- Freshen linens by hanging them out in the sun. This works for everything from your feather duvet and pillows to rugs and upholstery.

- Remove odors from laundry by adding vinegar into the washer where the fabric softener goes.

- When making bath bombs or cleaning bombs, sprinkle the leftovers onto your rugs and allow to sit for an hour before vacuuming. You can also add a few drops of essential oils to baking soda and sprinkle it on rugs if you haven't been making bombs.

- A little baking soda in the cat's litter box really helps with odors.

- In my home, I use white vinegar for cleaning pretty much everything. I keep a few bottles in the house and quickly spray sinks and surfaces to freshen them up. Doing this often becomes routine and less of a chore.

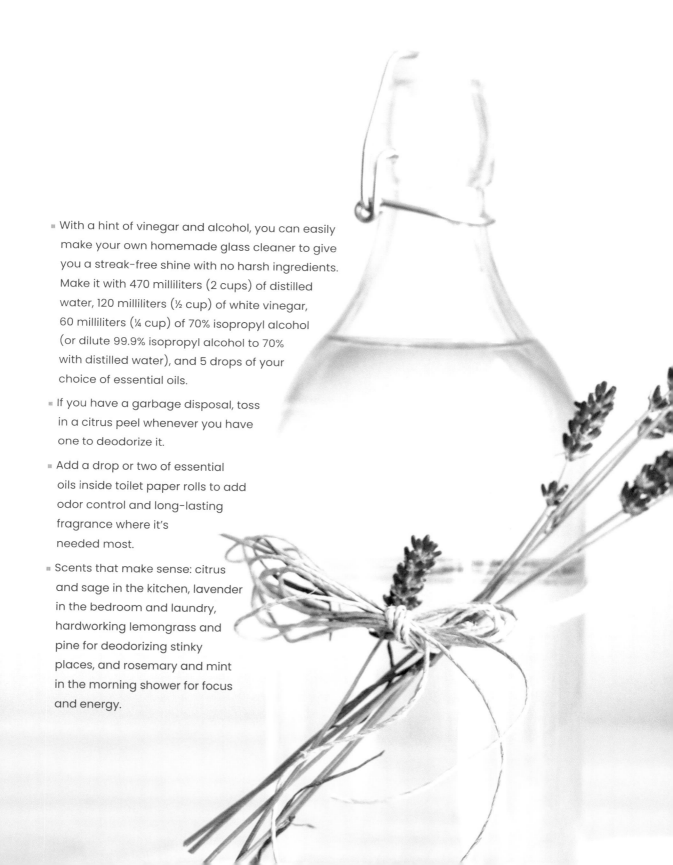

- With a hint of vinegar and alcohol, you can easily make your own homemade glass cleaner to give you a streak-free shine with no harsh ingredients. Make it with 470 milliliters (2 cups) of distilled water, 120 milliliters (½ cup) of white vinegar, 60 milliliters (¼ cup) of 70% isopropyl alcohol (or dilute 99.9% isopropyl alcohol to 70% with distilled water), and 5 drops of your choice of essential oils.

- If you have a garbage disposal, toss in a citrus peel whenever you have one to deodorize it.

- Add a drop or two of essential oils inside toilet paper rolls to add odor control and long-lasting fragrance where it's needed most.

- Scents that make sense: citrus and sage in the kitchen, lavender in the bedroom and laundry, hardworking lemongrass and pine for deodorizing stinky places, and rosemary and mint in the morning shower for focus and energy.

Herbal Appendix

There are many botanicals that can be used in these recipes, but some are powerhouses that serve many purposes. This is my list of go-to common herbs that will bring joy and healing into your life.

ALOE VERA (*ALOE BARBADENSIS*)

A skin-healing herb that can be grown as a houseplant. The gel extracted from fresh leaves is antimicrobial, skin-soothing, and wound-healing and can be used for burns, skin disorders, wounds, sunburns, frostbite, and chronic/acute dermatitis. (See pages 136, 138, and 149.)

BASIL (*OCIMUM BASILICUM*)

Aromatic, antimicrobial, and enlivening, basil is often used on skin to help repair, balance, and nourish skin, but it is also wonderful as a fresh-scented cleaner. (See page 141.)

BERGAMOT (*CITRUS BERGAMIA*)

Used for antibacterial and anti-inflammatory properties that help to calm skin. It also adds a pleasant floral citrus scent. (See pages 27, 71, and 141.)

CALENDULA (*CALENDULA OFFICINALIS*)

The most common healing herb for skin. The flowers are used to infuse oils for antiseptic, cell-repairing, and skin-soothing properties for treating bruises, burns, sores, and skin ulcers. A cornerstone skin-healing herb. (See pages 25, 31, 39, 51, and 101.)

COMFREY (*SYMPHYTUM OFFICINALE*)

A skin-healing herb used to treat wounds and pain topically. (See pages 25 and 35.)

DANDELION (*TARAXACUM OFFICINALE*)

Restorative, rejuvenating, and nutritive. The leaves, flowers, and roots are all edible and used in herbal recipes. (See page 59.)

ENGLISH LAVENDER (*LAVANDULA ANGUSTIFOLIA*)

Lavender is the scent of calmness and a top herb for skincare, aromatherapy, and cleaning. It contains aromatic, antimicrobial, analgesic, and relaxing compounds that help with sleep and relaxation, along with treating pain, wounds, bug bites, and fungal infections. (See pages 25, 27, 31, 35, 39, 43, 51, 71, 101, 105, 113, 129, 135, 149, 153, 157, and 180.)

GERMAN CHAMOMILE (*MATRICARIA CHAMOMILLA*)

Gentle enough to use on babies and makes a lovely cup of bedtime tea. Both flowers (primary) and leaves provide gentle yet powerful properties when added to tea, baths, and dream pillows. Anti-inflammatory when used topically for burns, rashes, and conjunctivitis. (See pages 25, 31, 39, and 101.)

HOPS (*HUMULUS LUPULUS*)

Used for skin inflammation, wrinkles, acne, and promoting sleep. This herb is relaxing, easing tension and insomnia. Note: avoid using with depression. (See pages 101 and 180.)

LEMON BALM (*MELISSA OFFICINALIS*)

The herb for little red spots. Use the leaves before flowering to infuse oils for treating bug bites, herpes/cold sores, and chicken pox. Use the leaves to infuse vinegar for cleaning for a lemony and uplifting scent. (See page 161.)

LEMONGRASS (*CYMBOPOGON* SPP.)

Aromatic and uplifting, the strong scent of lemongrass is a great deodorizer.
(See pages 71, 105, 129, 165, and 181.)

PEPPERMINT (*MENTHA X PIPERITA*)

Refreshing, deodorizing, and analgesic. The aromatic leaves and flowers are used for itching, inflamed skin, pain, and odor control. (See pages 25, 31, 35, 55, 63, 71, 101, 177, and 181.)

PINE (*PINUS* SPP.)

As an herb, pine has a fresh scent that is a natural decongestant, anti-inflammatory, antibacterial, and antimicrobial. Perfect for freshening up the house in cleaning recipes and holiday candles. (See pages 165 and 181.)

ROSE (*ROSA* SPP.)

Wonderful on the face since it helps reduce inflammation, wounds, wrinkles, and redness. Many parts are used, including the petals, leaves, and fruit (hips). Rose is astringent, analgesic, calming, aphrodisiac, and anti-inflammatory. (See pages 25, 27, 31, 39, 67, 71, and 129.)

ROSEMARY (*ROSMARINUS OFFICINALIS*)

The herb for healthy hair, fresh cleaning, and focus. The leaves are aromatic, circulatory stimulant, antimicrobial, and antioxidant, making it a very versatile herb. It also has an antibacterial quality. (See pages 35, 145, 169, and 181.)

SAGE (*SALVIA OFFICINALIS*)

Sage has been used for ages for its anti-inflammatory, antifungal, and antibacterial properties. It is wonderful as tea, in skincare, and as a cleaner. (See pages 25, 39, 161, and 181.)

TEA TREE (*MELALEUCA ALTERNIFOLIA*)

Its oil is an antifungal and antiseptic used for skin treatments as well as for cleaning and deodorizing. (See pages 135, 153, and 177.)

WITCH HAZEL (*HAMAMELIS* SPP.)

Prized for its anti-inflammatory and skincare properties, witch hazel also makes a great skin toner. (See pages 39, 136, 138, 149, 153, and 180.)

Resources

- American Botanical Council (online herbal resource): abc.herbalgram.org/site/PageServer?pagemane=Herbal%20_Library
- The Herbarium (membership site): herbarium.theherbalacademy.com
- Richters Herbs (sells plants, seeds, and herbs): richters.com
- Mountain Rose Herbs (bulk supplies): mountainroseherbs.com
- Rosemary Gladstar's The Science & Art of Herbalism training program (home study course): scienceandartofherbalism.com
- *Rosemary Gladstar's Herbal Recipes for Vibrant Health* by Rosemary Gladstar (paperback, 2008)
- *Alchemy of Herbs* by Rosalee de la Forêt (paperback, 2017)

Index

A

air-dry clay, 37

alkanet (Ratan Jot), 39

aloe vera, 136, 138, 149–150, 182

annatto seed powder, 39

anxiety, 10

aromatherapy, 27, 39, 71–72, 128–129, 135, 137, 184

B

baking sheet, 117–118

baking soda, 31, 39–40, 134, 177–178, 180

balms, 8, 19, 21, 54

basil (*Ocimum basilicum*), 141, 182

bath time, tips for, 75

beeswax, 16, 20, 22–23, 47–48, 51–52, 55–56, 80, 82–84

bergamot (*Citrus bergamia*), 141, 182

botanicals, 8, 11, 16, 19, 21–22, 24, 27–28, 75, 80, 180, 182

burlap bag, 29, 49

C

caffeine, 89

calendula (*Calendula officinalis*), 25, 51, 182

calendula-infused grapeseed oil, 51

calendula lotion bars, 51

calendula petals, 39–40, 51–53, 101

candle

  containers, 80

  cracks in a, 87

  issues in, 87

  safety, 80, 87

  scent, 85

  types of, 79

candle-making pitcher, 81

candle-making temperature, 84

carrier oils, 72

Castile soap, 141–142, 145–146, 165–166, 177–178

castor oil, 23, 55–56

chamomile, *see* German chamomile

cinnamon essential oil, 89

citric acid, 39–40, 135, 173–174, 177–178

citronella oil, 93–94

citrus, 27, 97–99, 101, 137–138, 141, 145, 181–182

cocoa butter, 16, 22–23, 43–44, 51–52, 55–56

cocoa powder, 39, 55–56

coffee bean massage bars, 47

comfrey (*Symphytum officinale*), 25, 35, 182

container candles, basic steps for, 86

cork sheet, 93–94

cornstarch, 39

craft paintbrush, 113

crayons, 83, 110

D

dandelion (*Taraxacum officinale*), 59, 60, 182

dead sea salts, 31

double boiler, 20–21, 55–56, 89–90, 93–94, 109–110, 113–114, 117–118

dried

   flowers, 31, 39, 71–72

   herbs, 21, 31, 39, 61

   spices, 31

E

electrical tape, 93–94

English lavender (*Lavandula angustifolia*), 25, 27, 43, 113, 135, 184

Epsom salt, 23, 27–28, 35–36, 39–40

equipment

   for home apothecary projects, 20

   for candle making, 81–82

   for soap and sanitizer projects, 138

essential oils, 22, 71, 85, 128, 137

essential oil scent blends, 129

eucalyptus essential oil, 35

expiration dates, 22, 138

F

floral bath bombs, 39–41

foot pain, 35

fragrance oils, 85

G

geranium, 39, 67, 71, 105, 129

German chamomile (*Matricaria chamomilla*), 25, 184

glass candle jar, 125

glass pot, 59–60

glue, 82, 84, 93–94, 105–106, 109–110, 113–114, 125–126

goat milk, 31

grapeseed oil, 23–24, 47–48, 51–52, 55, 72

green tea leaves, 31

ground oatmeal, 31

H

healing power, 9–10, 16, 22, 24

health issues, personal, 128, 138

heartfelt connections, 11

heating methods, for herb-infused oils, 24

herb benefits, 25

herb blends, 31, 101

herb-infused oils, 24–25

herbal foot soak, 35

herbal teas, 64

Himalayan pink salt, 31, 67–68

honey, 23, 59–60, 82–83

hops (*Humulus lupulus*), 101, 184

hot glue gun, 82, 89, 93–94, 105, 109, 113, 125

hydrogen peroxide, 135

I

isopropyl alcohol, 134–135, 153, 155, 157, 165, 181

K

kitchen scale, 20, 47, 51, 59–60, 67–68, 81, 117, 121, 125

L

lavender, *see* English lavender

lavender buds, 27, 101, 135, 180

lavender essential oil, 27, 35, 43, 129, 135, 149, 153, 157, 180

lemon, 27, 97, 129, 135, 157, 161, 169, 184

lemon balm (*Melissa officinalis*), 161, 184

lemon essential oil, 129, 157, 169

lemongrass (*Cymbopogon* spp.), 165, 184

lemongrass essential oil, 129, 165

lime, 27, 97, 129, 145

lotion bar, 53

M

mandarin orange, 71, 105

measurements, 9, 20, 81, 138

measuring cups, 138, 145, 149, 153, 157, 161, 165

melting ingredients, 19

   double boiler method, 21

   microwave method, 21

metal tray, 93, 109–110

milk, powdered, 31

molds, 20

N

notes, fragrance, 71

O

oils, *see* essential oils; fragrance oils; plant oils

old towel, 89, 93, 109, 113, 125

olive oil, 22, 24, 59–60, 141

orange essential oil, 101, 129, 153

P

paper cup, 82, 86, 89–90, 93–94, 97, 101, 125

paper tea filters, 31

paprika, 39

paraffin wax, 82–83

patchouli, 71, 105, 129

peppermint (*Mentha* x *piperita*), 25, 55, 63, 177, 185

peppermint essential oil, 55, 63, 177

pine (*Pinus* spp.), 165, 185

plant oils, 16, 22, 23, 24, 128, 135

    castor oil, 23

    cocoa butter, 23

    coconut oil, 23

    grapeseed oil, 23

    olive oil, 23

    sweet almond oil, 23

R

roasted coffee beans, 47, 91

rose (*Rosa* spp.), 25, 27, 185

rosemary (*Rosmarinus officinalis*), 145, 169, 185

rosemary essential oil, 35, 145, 169

rose petals, 25, 27, 39, 67–68

rubber gloves, 125–126

S

safety, 80, 138

safflower powder, 39

sage (*Salvia officinalis*), 25, 161, 185

sage essential oil, 161–162

salt, 23, 27–29, 31–32, 39–40, 67–68, 173–175

sanitizers, 130–137, 139, 143, 145, 149, 151, 155, 157, 163, 165, 171

self-esteem, building, 10

sewing machine, 31–32

shelf life, 22, 138

silicone ice cube trays, 20, 43, 97–98, 177–178

silicone molds, 101

silicone sealer, 93–94

soaps, 8, 130–139, 141, 143, 155, 157, 159, 161, 163, 165

soy wax, 82–85, 87, 89–90, 93–94, 97–98, 101–102, 105, 109, 113, 125–126

spirulina, 39, 63–64

spray bottle, 39–40, 153, 163, 165–166, 173–174, 177–178

stress, 10, 12, 113

sugar, 22, 59–60, 63–64

T

tea tree (*Melaleuca alternifolia*), 135, 177, 185

tea tree oil, 135, 153

thermometer, 81, 89, 93–94, 105–106, 109, 113–114, 125

toilet bombs, 177

tub tea, 31

turmeric, 31, 39

V

vegetable glycerin, 136, 153

vinegar, 128, 134–135, 137, 161–163, 169–170, 173–175, 180–181

virgin coconut oil, 23, 51, 63

vitamin E oil, 22, 149–150

vodka, 135, 165

W

wax adhesive, 82, 86, 89–90, 105–106, 109–110, 113–114, 125–126

wax melts, 79–81, 97–99, 101–102

wellness, 8, 10–11, 128

wicks, 84

witch hazel (*Hamamelis* spp.), 39, 136, 149, 185

wooden clothespins, 33, 82

wooden scoop, 35

Notes

Use these pages to jot down your personal scent blends, recipe experimentation, notes about when your products will expire, etc.

BETTER DAY BOOKS®

HAPPY · CREATIVE · CURATED

Business is personal at Better Day Books. We were founded on the belief that all people are creative and that making things by hand is inherently good for us. It's important to us that you know how much we appreciate your support. The book you are holding in your hands was crafted with the artistic passion of the author and brought to life by a team of wildly enthusiastic creatives who believed it could inspire you. If it did, please drop us a line and let us know about it. Connect with us on Instagram, post a photo of your art, and let us know what other creative pursuits you are interested in learning about. It all matters to us. You're kind of a big deal.

it's a good day to have a better day!®

www.betterdaybooks.com

better_day_books